ROCK 'N' ROLL
HEAVEN

ROCK 'N' ROLL HEAVEN

PHILIP JACOBS

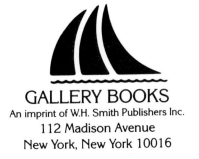

GALLERY BOOKS
An imprint of W.H. Smith Publishers Inc.
112 Madison Avenue
New York, New York 10016

A QUINTET BOOK
produced for
GALLERY BOOKS
An imprint of W.H. Smith Publishers Inc.
112 Madison Avenue
New York, New York 10016

ISBN 0–8317–7414–2

This book was designed and produced by
Quintet Publishing Limited
6 Blundell Street
London N7 9BH

Creative Director: Peter Bridgewater
Art Director: Ian Hunt
Designers: James Lawrence, Stuart Walden
Artwork: Danny McBride
Project Editor: Shaun Barrington
Picture Researcher: Norman Jopling

Typeset in Great Britain by
Central Southern Typesetters, Eastbourne
Manufactured in Hong Kong by
Regent Publishing Services Limited
Printed in Hong Kong by
Leefung-Asco Printers Limited

CONTENTS

INTRODUCTION 6

ELVIS PRESLEY 12

BUDDY HOLLY 18

BILL HALEY 22

EDDIE COCHRANE 25

GENE VINCENT 29

BOBBY DARIN 31

RICK NELSON 34

ROY ORBISON 36

SAM COOKE 39

OTIS REDDING 42

MARVIN GAYE 44

DENNIS WILSON 47

JIMI HENDRIX 51

JANIS JOPLIN 54

JIM MORRISON 58

BRIAN JONES 60

JOHN LENNON 63

KEITH MOON 68

DUANE ALLMAN 71

BOB MARLEY 73

HARRY CHAPIN 76

JIM CROCE 78

MARC BOLAN 80

ANDY GIBB 84

LYNYRD SKYNYRD 86

ALSO IN ROCK 'N' ROLL HEAVEN 88

INDEX 94

ACKNOWLEDGEMENTS 96

INTRODUCTION

If it's true that 'Whom the gods love die young' then the gods must be a real bunch of rock'n'roll fanatics. From which other profession have they taken so many top figures so young? Not from politics, science or sport, have they plucked even a quarter of the numbers they've taken from the rock world.

No area of rock music is immune. Judging by the characters who are up there, the heavenly crowd like a lot of soul (Sam Cooke, Otis Redding, Marvin Gaye); some deep Southern Boogie (Duane Allman, Ronnie Van Zant and Steve Gaines); a smattering of sixties West Coast (Mama Cass, Ron 'Pigpen' McKernan); English rock (John Lennon, Keith Moon, Brian Jones); even a pinch of clean-cut male vocals (Ricky Nelson, Bobby Darin).

RIGHT: *The Carpenters performing on stage. Fatalities in the rock world were drawn from all areas of the music.*

LEFT: *Frankie Lymon. After a brief spell of success in his early teens, Lymon languished in obscurity for nearly ten years before his death in 1968.*

ABOVE: *Elvis Presley with Barbara Stanwyck in the film 'Roustabout'. It has consistently been the top performers in each field of music who have gone before their time.*

But the favourite sound in Celestial City must be fifties rock'n'roll, the sound that started it all off. Elvis is up there – it took some time but they got him in the end – Buddy Holly was taken at 22, Eddie Cochran at 21, Bill Haley and Gene Vincent both ascended ahead of schedule. The only majors figures from the Golden Age of rock'n' roll to elude the Grim Reaper are Jerry Lee Lewis, Little Richard and Fats Domino.

Sometimes the stars arrive in heaven of their own accord, other times the gods are more active in making the arrangements. One of their favourite ways of recruiting members for the rock band on high is to grab them when they're already in the air. Airplane crashes account for the deaths of many rock music figures including Buddy Holly, Ritchie Valens, Otis Redding, Ricky Nelson, Jim Croce, Ronnie Van Zant and Steve Gaines.

Motorcycle and car crashes are not as popular as the airborne variety but nonetheless, Eddie Cochran, Duane Allman, Harry Chapin and Marc Bolan were all taken this way.

One route by which rock stars need no help in taking the stairway to heaven is drugs. Here they can make it alone quite nicely and there is no

ABOVE: *Jimi Hendrix (centre) with The Experience (left: Mitch Mitchell right: Noel Redding) – Hendrix burst on to rock's centre stage in 1967, burned brightly for 3 years, then died, still at the peak of his invention.*

shortage of people who have succeeded in doing just that – Jimi Hendrix, Janis Joplin, Frankie Lymon, Paul Kossoff, two Pretenders and Sid Vicious all stumbled through the Pearly Gates in various states of narcotic intoxication.

A more low-key method of conscripting rock'n'roll choristers is through illness. Several stars like Roy Orbison, Gene Vincent, Bill Haley, Mama Cass and Bob Marley died from natural causes.

The celestial taste in individual rock stars is not infallible, but in many cases it must be said that they have got the right man. Who was the best guitarist on earth? Jimi Hendrix. The best singer? Elvis Presley. And so it goes on – the gods have consistently picked out the best and left the others for us. If they had to have just one reggae star who would it be? Bob Marley. Which one of the Beatles would they choose? John Lennon. If they could only have two soul singers they couldn't do better than Sam Cooke and Otis Redding.

If the gods have shown general good taste in picking rock stars, it must also be said that their timing is not perfect. Elvis Presley was at his peak from 1954 to 1957 yet the whole of the sixties and nearly all of the seventies went by before the deities realized he was the King. By the time they caught him, he was in such bad shape that he'd hardly have been able to muster a wiggle from his once notorious pelvis.

Buddy Holly was nearer his peak when he was inducted into the ultimate

ABOVE: *English Rock 'n' Roller Billy Fury. Performers from both sides of the Atlantic were chosen to play in Rock 'n' Roll heaven.*

Hall of Fame at 22 and poor Eddie Cochran was only 21. The youngest member though – and he joined before he was even allowed to vote – was 17 year old Ritchie Valens.

In general though, the stars were in decline by the time they were taken from us and for this we should be thankful – that particularly cruel and greedy gratitude that only a fan can feel. In this book then, we say thanks by celebrating the lives and achievements of those whose echos still ring in the palladiums and amphitheatres of rock'n'roll heaven.

LEFT: *James Honeyman-Scott, guitarist and one of the founders of The Pretenders. The trend for rock stars to die young continued into the 1980s. Honeyman-Scott died in 1982.*

HIT RECORDINGS	
1956	HEARTBREAK HOTEL
1956	I WANT YOU, I NEED YOU
1956	DON'T BE CRUEL
1956	HOUND DOG
1956	LOVE ME
1956	LOVE ME TENDER
1957	TOO MUCH
1957	ALL SHOOK UP
1957	LET ME BE YOUR TEDDY BEAR
1957	LOVING YOU
1957	JAILHOUSE ROCK
1957	TREAT ME NICE
1958	DON'T
1958	ONE NIGHT
1959	A BIG HUNK 'O LOVE
1960	STUCK ON YOU
1960	IT'S NOW OR NEVER
1960	ARE YOU LONESOME TONIGHT
1961	SURRENDER
1962	RETURN TO SENDER
1963	DEVIL IN DISGUISE
1963	BOSSA NOVA BABY
1965	CRYING IN THE CHAPEL
1969	IN THE GHETTO
1969	SUSPICIOUS MINDS
1970	DON'T CRY DADDY
1970	THE WONDER OF YOU
1972	BURNING LOVE

There is no doubt which star shines brightest in the Rock'n'Roll firmament – Elvis Aaron Presley. His looks alone could have guaranteed him a career as a teen idol. 'Teenagers' had just started to make themselves felt in society and after the death of James Dean in 1955, they were left without a role model. Elvis came along just in time, he had the smouldering good looks, the rebellious clothes and a sexual arrogance that was missing in Dean. Before he even sang a note, he was the perfect teen idol.

When he did sing, it wasn't just his lips that moved, it was his whole body; it was as if he was on fire with the power of music. To see him perform live – in his early days at least – was to be electrified by the energy which surged through him and into the crowd. Agents and managers are always

RIGHT: *Said to be 'the most photographed face of the twentieth century', Elvis' looks and attitude were almost as influential as his music and continue to fascinate . . .*

BELOW: *The Hollywood years: the mid 1960s 'Elvis movie machine' is now considered the nadir of his career.*

ABOVE: *Elvis' Bedroom,
1955, in the Memphis home
he bought for his parents.
All pink and blue . . .*

simulating scenes of mass hysteria to hype an act but there was nothing simulated about Elvis' performance as reports from recording sessions of the 1950's confirm; he swayed as wildly in the studio as he did on the stage.

Elvis was born in Tupelo, Mississippi in 1935, at a time when the South was still suffering from the effects of the Depression. Work was scarce and his father Vernon was regularly unemployed. In an effort to improve their prospects the Presleys moved to Memphis, Tennessee where Elvis became a teenager. He was a combination of two opposites, shy on the one hand and outrageous on the other. People thought he was a hoodlum as he walked through the streets of Memphis in his flashy pink jackets with long piled-up, greased–back hair. Yet when he talked he was polite and nervous, he didn't smoke or drink, he called his elders 'Sir' or 'Ma'am', and, in the age of 'Rebel Without a Cause', respected his parents.

His recordings though, were anything but polite. In the first recordings he made for Sun Records all his youthful energy exploded into wild anarchic

OPPOSITE ABOVE: *On stage
1957: the archetype of the
guitar-toutin' rock star. In
fact, Presley used his
instrument percussively on
stage, despite being a
powerful rhythm guitarist.
In the background are the
Jordanaires road group,
and note the 1957 amp!*

OPPOSITE BELOW: *Goofin'
off at a drumkit during an
early RCA Nashville
session.*

music. It wasn't the fact that he was recording blues that was unusual, it was the incredible manic drive that he put into it. Furthermore, country songs were given the same treatment, so 'Blue Moon Of Kentucky' is as hot as 'That's Alright Mama'. No one had sung like this before and when Elvis actually started doing it, he was only messing around. He actually thought of himself as a slow ballad singer and did songs like 'Old Shep' – sentimental tear jerkers that would have pleased his fans' parents and probably their grandparents as well. It was Sun Records boss Sam Phillips who realized Elvis had hit upon something big and encouraged him to continue in that direction.

White pop music of the time had become very slick and appealed more to adults than kids. Elvis, who had grown up listening to black radio stations, brought the raw directness of R&B into the white music field and energized the young. R&B wasn't arranged and orchestrated like white popular music, there were no witty lyrics, just clear statements of basic feelings. The very term 'rock'n'roll' was not one, but two black euphemisms for the sexual act. With a young, mean-looking leader and a music of their own, the teen revolution was on.

One of the men most instrumental in taking the new music into the popular mainstream was Colonel Parker. He was a small-time country music manager who had seen Elvis perform and was astonished by the reaction of a crowd that was watching him. The Colonel had never seen anything like it – after all, country music was a relatively subdued affair – but Elvis was driving the crowd wild and Parker was convinced that Elvis could be a national phenomenon. After becoming Elvis' manager he moved the singer from the small Sun Record Label to the big international company, RCA.

With RCA's national distribution and television exposure, Elvis became a sensation. As well as being popular he was also very controversial; his rebellious look, his singing black music and his uninhibited body movements, all enraged conservative America, and sent his popularity with the teenagers soaring.

His RCA recordings of 1956 like 'Heartbreak Hotel', 'Blue Suede Shoes' and 'Hound Dog' show authority and control in his singing, but there is still phenomenal power and considerable maturity from someone who was still only 21 years old. Moving into 1957 Elvis slowed down. His own choice of songs for recordings were mainly country and gospel numbers, the only hard rock'n'roll he recorded being from the films 'Loving You' and 'Jailhouse Rock'. But whether he rocked hard or soft his popularity continued unabated.

Then in 1958 Elvis surprised everyone by joining the army. There was no necessity for him to do so – celebrities had always found ways of avoiding the draft – so this was obviously part of the Colonel's plan. It didn't seem to make sense though. How could Parker withdraw the world's most popular singer from public life at the peak of his success? The truth was that at heart Parker distrusted rock'n'roll; he thought it would fade out and he didn't want his protégé to fade with it. He was determined that Elvis should appeal to everyone, not just the youngsters, but to adults as well and by sending him into the army, he could change Elvis from a dangerous rebel to a good, law abiding citizen.

By this time Elvis himself had completed a full artistic life. You can hear his voice changing over the years as he matures and develops and by 1958 he seemed to have done all that was possible within the confines of rock'n' roll. From there on there would be nothing new to do; all that would be left would be weak copies or ridiculous travesties of his earlier work. Before going into the army he was an artist – after coming out he was an entertainer. Colonel Parker's plan seemed to be working fine.

For a while it looked as though the movies might provide an artistic challenge for Elvis – after all, he had undeniable charisma and had proved in films like 'Jailhouse Rock' and 'King Creole' that he could act. Unfor-

Elvis tackles 'Love Me Tender' on the keyboards in 1956, and often accompanied himself on piano for his favourite gospel numbers.

tunately, it was not to be, Colonel Parker had found that vacuous musicals were the most profitable movies to make; they could be churned out quickly and provide a ready source of songs for album release. While the Presley image in the films was wholesome and lovable, and his good looks ensured that he was still a big hit with the women, his talent was sorely wasted – not only in acting, but in singing as well. Consider these song titles from some of the movies he was in – 'Shake That Tambourine' 'Singing Tree' 'Old MacDonald Had A Farm' 'A Whistling Tune' and 'There's No Room To Rhumba In A Sports Car', they are a good gauge of how bad the films they appeared in actually were.

The only way was down. He did try to make a comeback at the end of the 1960's when his film career was over. His television '68 Special shows a man straining for – and sometimes reaching – heights that were effortlessly attainable for the young Elvis. The divorce of his wife Priscilla in 1972 seemed to be the end for Elvis. Priscilla wasn't just any woman, she was the custom-made Presley bride. They first met in Germany when Elvis was posted over there with the army and she was just 14. Elvis took over her education, apparently grooming her for the marriage which finally took place in 1966. Family life was always important to Elvis and with his mother dying in 1958 and then Priscilla leaving there was nothing to hold on to. Elvis abandoned himself to the land of drug-induced oblivion.

This was yet another of Elvis' contradictions. He wholeheartedly disapproved of the fashion in the 1960's for taking drugs, and although he took huge amounts of them himself, they were always prescribed. His drugs were not the fashionable ones – cannabis, LSD or cocaine, but legal drugs, Dilaudid, Placidyl, Darvon, Tuinal, Valium, Eskotrol and many, many others. Deep in the grips of a self-destructive depression, Elvis was feeding a voracious appetite for food and sex as well as drugs. His drug habit started with uppers to keep him awake through tours, then downers to help him sleep, then more uppers to help him lose weight, then more tranquillisers, pain killers, sedatives – the list spiralled alarmingly.

All these drugs affected both Presley's mind and body; He believed at times that he could control the weather and heal the sick. But if drugs kept him out of the real world mentally, Colonel Parker kept him isolated physically. Asked in the early days if he planned to get married, Elvis replied 'Why get a cow when you can get free milk?' Parker immediately withdrew him from all public appearances, the only image that people would have of Presley from now on would be the image that Parker himself created. So effective was he in doing this that it was only after Elvis's death that people realized that he even took drugs.

There is no shortage of rumours claiming that Elvis is still alive, but the theory that Elvis faked his own death would be a bit easier to believe were it not for the fact that he nearly died several times before 16 August 1977. Only expert help kept him from an earlier death on those occasions. People who were with him at the time often said that he was wilfully self destructive, as if he almost wanted to die; a sad end for pop music's most perfect star.

ABOVE TOP: *Despite overwhelming pressures, Elvis maintained a punishing touring schedule even during the mid 1970s when his physical deterioration was giving severe cause for concern.*

ABOVE: *Elvis had always been moderately self-indulgent, but it was the break-up of his marriage to Priscilla in 1972 that tipped the scales towards self-destruction.*

1936
BUDDY HOLLY

1959

HIT RECORDINGS	
1957	THAT'LL BE THE DAY
1957	PEGGY SUE
1958	OH BOY
1958	MAYBE BABY
1959	IT DOESN'T MATTER ANYMORE

Buddy Holly was an original. He had his own way of singing, his own style of music and his own way of writing songs. In an industry where about 1 percent lead and 99 percent follow, he was a leader. Like Elvis Presley, he took the raw material of country and blues and fused them into a personal style that could score on the worldwide pop market. Unlike Presley, though, his death came only two years after his first hit.

Music had always interested Buddy, and he pursued his interest with singular purpose. His seriousness even at an early age amazed his musical schoolfriends, who often found themselves being reproached for not playing things the way he had told them. Drawn by his enthusiasm though, the

BELOW: *Buddy Holly and The Crickets. Holly began performing without his glasses, but after dropping his pick one night, and having to get down on hands and knees to find it, he decided to wear his glasses from then on.*

BELOW: *Buddy was playing music at an early age. He had his own radio show while he was still at school.*

friends stayed with Buddy and together the young band played wherever they could – at supermarket openings, school functions, parties. They even managed to get their own local radio show, named after the two singers in the group – 'The Buddy and Bob Show'.

The radio slot paid off, leading to better concert opportunities and at one show a Nashville talent scout saw Holly's band. A recording contract was offered, but for Buddy alone; he wanted to go but was unsure about breaking up his partnership with Bob Montgomery. Bob though, knew that the opportunity was too good to miss and finally convinced Holly to go.

Nashville was, and still is, the home of country music, but it wasn't so at home with rock'n'roll. The new musical craze was threatening the livelihood of many people working in Nashville so was viewed with a mixture of suspicion and loathing. When he arrived, Holly found the traditionalism of the Decca establishment stifling as the people in charge of his recording career were old hands who did not want to be told what to do by a Lubbock greenhorn. They wanted to process Holly like they had countless other country singers, irrespective of his originality.

Buddy had put together a new band for the recording sessions and wanted to feature original material. Suggesting to drummer Jerry Allison that they write a song one night, the drummer replied 'That'll Be The Day' and Buddy's eyes lit up. Together they wrote the song which was later to become so famous, and excitedly took it to Decca. Decca recorded it without enthusiasm and refused to release it as a single on the grounds that it wasn't good enough. The time had come for Holly and Decca to part.

There was a producer in Clovis, New Mexico, called Norman Petty who Buddy had heard was sympathetic to new talent. He could hear something original in Holly's music and was prepared to put in the time and work to bring it out. Holly could hardly have found a better place to go. Petty loved 'That'll Be The Day' and wanted to record it immediately. He did, and made a far better recording of it than the Nashville version, but when they came to release it, they had a problem. In the contract Holly had signed with Decca was a clause preventing him from re-recording any of his material with another company for five years. This meant that if 'That'll Be The Day' was to come out under Holly's name they would have to wait four years. If it came out under another name, however, it could be released immediately. And so the Crickets were born.

'That'll Be The Day' proved to be the hit they all knew it would be, reaching No. 1 in September 1957. The Crickets had become famous and demand arose for them to tour, to record more and to appear on television. A new song 'Peggy Sue' recorded with the Crickets came out under Buddy Holly's name alone and when that became a big hit Holly effectively had two separate recording careers. To prove that the Crickets were also still going strong, their next single 'Oh Boy' repeated the success of 'That'll Be The Day'. As 1957 drew to a close they were at their peak of success.

Most of 1958 saw them touring. The Crickets had played widely in the United States but had not ventured abroad until now. The first stop was

Buddy Holly and the Crickets set the trend for the growth of the self-contained rock group, but their 1958 UK tour saw them planted firmly back in the British music hall tradition.

Australia. Also on the bill was wild man of rock'n'roll Jerry Lee Lewis and the then 15-year-old Paul Anka who, on the strength of his big Australian hit 'Diana', was top of the bill. Most acclaim though, went neither to Anka or Jerry Lee Lewis, but to the Crickets.

Reaction in Great Britain was similar and many young British kids had their first experience of live rock'n'roll from this tour. In one audience was a 16-year-old Paul McCartney, who from that day on remained a lifelong fan of Holly's and always named him as a profound influence and inspiration.

Holly and the Crickets returned to the United States where Buddy met, and fell in love with, Maria Elena Santiago. Buddy was so taken with her and so sure they would be right together that he proposed to her on their first date – and she accepted. Although the marriage was a good one, it tended to weaken the ties that held the Crickets together.

Maria was a cosmopolitan New Yorker and Buddy began to spend all his time with her there. The city's music publishers and recording studios also attracted Buddy and the more time he spent in New York, the more he wanted to move there. His records weren't selling as well as they had done and he thought it was time to break from Norman Petty. He suggested this to the Crickets who were not convinced, and the band split.

Buddy began to record in New York, and it was here, without the Crickets, that he began to think about using an orchestra as backing. No rock'n'roller had ever sung with an orchestra before, so Holly was taking a chance, but he knew that strings would sound good on the slow numbers and they might even open up a larger audience for him. He recorded 'It Doesn't Matter Anymore' in 1959 and scored his biggest hit since 'Oh Boy'.

But despite his recent success, Buddy Holly was not a rich man. Most of the money he'd earned was still with Norman Petty in Clovis. To keep himself going until his earnings with Petty could be legally worked out, Holly was forced to tour through the winter. It was a wretched tour; the stars, who included Ritchie Valens, Dion And The Belmonts and Waylon Jennings were all frozen, tired and dispirited as they huddled up in the tour bus. Buddy decided to charter a plane and fly to the next venue so as to get a good night's sleep before going to the ballroom for the concert.

When others heard about the plane, there was considerable jostling for the other seats. Waylon Jennings gave his seat to J P Richardson – the Big Bopper and Tommy Allsup gave his seat to Ritchie Valens. The plane was to be flown by a young pilot who had passed his exams for visual flying but had failed his instruments exams. The conditions were such that instruments were needed almost as soon as the plane took off. Eight miles later it smashed into the ground killing all on board on impact. Buddy Holly was 22 and Richie Valens was 17.

The influence of Buddy Holly was enormous, some people even credit the classic rock band line up of two guitars, bass and drums to him. Furthermore, with his ordinary looks and trademark glasses, he continues to give hope to people everywhere who think that talent is more important than packaging and hype.

The Crickets: Holly (left) with drummer Jerry Allison (above) and bassist Joe B. Maudlin. This trio toured the UK thrilling fans with their new power-trio format.

ABOVE TOP: *The Big Bopper (J. P. Richardson) signs autographs on Dick Clark's 'American Bandstand', after performing his hit 'Chantilly Lace' in 1958.*

ABOVE: *The wreckage of the plane in which not only Buddy Holly, but Ritchie Valens (right) and The Big Bopper (bottom) were also killed.*

BILL HALEY

HIT RECORDINGS

1953	CRAZY MAN CRAZY
1954	SHAKE RATTLE AND ROLL
1955	ROCK AROUND THE CLOCK
1956	SEE YOU LATER ALLIGATOR

There are many contenders for the title 'The Man Who Started Rock'n'Roll' and one of the most serious of them is William Haley Jr. This chubby, smiling performer always suffers when being compared to the younger, more dynamic Elvis, but he has to his credit one or two genuine rock'n'roll recordings made before Elvis even started performing.

Born in Michigan on 6 July, 1925, Bill Haley stumbled upon rock'n'roll by accident. Like many of the performers who eventually became rockers, he was originally a country singer. He and his Saddlemen performed in cowboy boots, hats and neck scarves, singing country standards of the day. One of the songs in their set though was 'Rock The Joint' – a relentless blues number that they used as an opener. It always drove the crowd wild but was viewed almost as a joke by the band who then reverted to their normal Country and Western repertoire.

Bill Haley and The Comets: they stumbled upon Rock 'n' Roll by accident.

Gradually though, other prototype rock'n'roll numbers were added to the set, and when released on record they caused a considerable stir. One song in particular, 'Crazy Man Crazy' seemed to catch on with the youngsters who were coming in increasing numbers to see him. After it became a hit, the cowboy trappings were discarded and the Saddlemen became the Comets.

In 1954 came Haley's big moment, the moment when rock history was made with the recording 'Rock Around The Clock'. It was custom written for Bill Haley and the Comets and for the new fans of rock'n'roll. It contains the word 'Rock' 34 times, and the chorus: 'We're gonna rock around the clock tonight, we're gonna rock, rock, rock, 'til broad daylight, we're gonna rock gonna rock around the clock tonight' makes it impossible not to rock.

This surefire hit song had to be recorded right, and it was. The arrangement was tight, each instrument adding to the drive of the rhythm, and the recording is so clear you can pick out every instrument – the slapping bass, the shotgun drumming, the riffing sax; everything comes up as clear as the day it was played. And this perfect rock'n'roll number was recorded four months before Elvis Presley had even started recording.

In the two years before Elvis became big, Haley was the King of Rock'n' Roll, he had hits in Britain and Australia and seemed to monopolize the rebellious teen audience of the world. When Elvis arrived, however, Haley was in trouble. The fans could identify with the image of Elvis – his clothes, his youth, his arrogance, while Haley was a respectably married, middle-aged entertainer. It is said that friends were not allowed to mention Presley's name in Haley's presence.

But even if Haley couldn't compete with Elvis image-wise, he might still have been able to turn out good records if he hadn't discovered that more money could be made writing songs than performing them. He and the Comets busily began writing without realizing that the money would only come if the songs were successful. Theirs were not, and by releasing poor songs, they were just driving their fans to Elvis.

Haley now thought about wooing the older market. After all, he had started as an all-round entertainer, why should he just concentrate on kids? His recordings of songs like 'Aint Misbehaving', 'Sweet Sue Just You' and 'Dinah', though, wooed neither kids nor adults.

It looked like desperation when the Comets promoted the twist as the craze to replace rock'n'roll. 'Florida Twist' was an instrumental with hardly any contribution from Haley on it but to everyone's surprise it hit big in Mexico. The Comets packed their bags and shot off to Mexico City where American hits were hastily translated into Spanish for the new audience. Let's Twist became 'Mas Twist', Green Door, 'Puerta Verde' and 'When The Saints Go Marching In', 'La Marcha De Los Santos'.

Back home, however, they had no success at all. Their attempts to cash in on the twist craze had failed, and with no money coming in from recordings, the Comets had to keep touring to survive. This proved too much for the band members, who in most cases had families to support and didn't

ABOVE: *Although their support came largely from the teenagers, it was some years since The Comets had seen their own teenage days. From left to right: Rudy Pompelli, Al Rex, John Grande, Bill Haley, Francis Beecher, Ralph Jones and Billy Williams.*

23

LEFT: *When times got hard for the band, The Comets left Haley – some for other bands and others for normal day jobs. Haley continued alone, always finding a local pick up group who could back him up.*

like spending the whole year away from them. One by one they deserted Haley, some staying in the music business and others returning to factory jobs.

Reckless spending was beginning to take its toll on Haley, he was unable to pay bills and finally his home 'Melody Manor' was taken from him. 'Melody Manor' was Haley's 'Graceland', a symbol of his achievement and it must have hurt him dearly to lose it. The final blow came when his wife left him. Without a band, a home or a wife, Haley hit rock bottom.

The first sign of a change for the better was the return of one of his Comets – saxophone player Rudy Pompelli, a devoted friend who was to help Haley considerably in the years to come. The real piece of luck though, was a worldwide revival of interest in rock'n'roll. Music in the late 1960's had become self-indulgent, and young people pined for the simplicity and danceability of rock'n'roll. Bill Haley was only too glad to supply it.

Although the heights of his 1950's fame would never be regained, Haley and Pompelli could still earn a living playing their old hits. It was hard though, and Haley increasingly turned to drink. When Rudy Pompelli died of cancer in 1976, it was the end, Haley had nothing left but the past. In the five years leading up to his death in 1981 he became unpredictable. The once wholesome entertainer began to behave badly under the influence of drink with tales of him physically attacking audiences, taking his clothes off on stage and habitually abusing friends who tried hard to help him. He died at home, alone, of a heart attack in February 1981.

1938
EDDIE COCHRAN

1960

Eddie Cochran started off as one of Elvis' brightest pupils, then came into his own with several self-written classics of rock'n'roll. Elvis used songs from a variety of sources, but none were true teenage songs. Efforts like 'Let Me Be Your Teddy Bear' were contrived affairs from professional songwriters pandering to the teenage audience. Chuck Berry also sang about teenage life but when he wrote his classic 'Schooldays' he was in his thirties. Eddie Cochran by contrast never lived past twenty-one.

Although he was born in Oklahoma City, Oklahoma, Cochran started his musical career in California. His family had moved there in 1949 when he was 11 and he learnt to play the guitar the following year. His first professional job came in 1954 as guitarist for singer Hank Cochran. Although the two were not related, they capitalized on the fact that they shared the same name and toured the South West states as the Cochran brothers. Originally

HIT RECORDINGS	
SUMMERTIME BLUES	1958
C'MON EVERYBODY	1959
THREE STEPS TO HEAVEN	1960

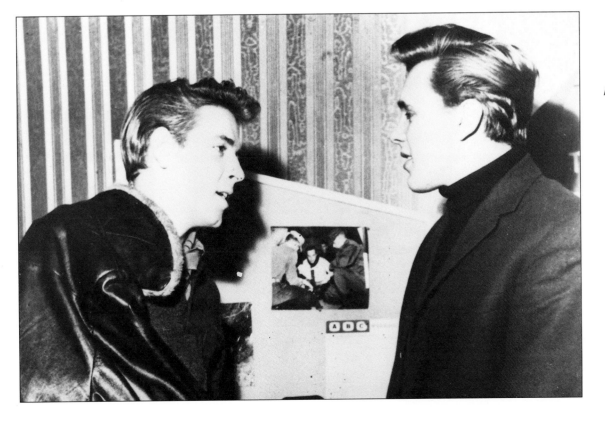

LEFT: *Eddie Cochran was one of the musicians responsible for bringing Rock 'n' Roll to Great Britain. Here he is with English rocker Billy Fury.*

playing hillbilly material at fairs and dances, their music was to change drastically after they saw Elvis Presley singing in Dallas in 1955.

The rockabilly bug hit Eddie hard. He added a drummer and pianist to the duo but Hank was none too pleased about the change and left the group in 1956. Eddie found a new partner in songwriter Jerry Capehart. The two had met in a music store, Jerry asking Eddie if he'd record one of his tunes and it was a partnership that would produce most of Cochran's biggest hits.

In 1956 Eddie was 18, he had absorbed the rockabilly sound and, like Buddy Holly, he was committed to making quality recordings. He knew that musical ability was nothing without solid material so his first priority was to get good songs, and with the help of Jerry Capehart he was able to produce some of the most enduring songs in all rock'n'roll.

Capehart was also an astute businessman, and was able to secure a publishing deal and then a contract with recording company Liberty who

RIGHT: *Eddie in 'The Girl Can't Help It' (1957), a film which also included performances by Little Richard, Fats Domino, Gene Vincent and Julie London.*

LEFT: *By 1959 Eddie was expanding the boundaries of rock 'n' roll with songs like 'Summertime Blues' and his swinging version of R & B star Ray Charles' 'Hallelujah I Love Her So'.*

put Eddie into the 1956 film, 'The Girl Can't Help It'. This – the best of all the rock'n'roll films of the 1950's – also contains performances by Little Richard, Fats Domino, Gene Vincent and Julie London, but Cochran stands proud among the giants, delivering the frantic rockabilly racer 'Twenty Flight Rock'. The sound of raw rockabilly though, was too rough for the pop mainstream and like Elvis Presley, Eddie had to sweeten it up a bit for his next release. 'Sittin' In The Balcony' was a slow smoocher and it made the Top 20 in 1957, but Cochran did not want to become a ballad singer and was determined to put the power of rockabilly into a pop setting without losing any of its fire. In 1958 he did just that.

'Summertime Blues' was not only a musical success, it was also a lyrical success. Cochran and Capehart had writen a chronicle of the problems facing a teenager in the late 1950's. In the song Eddie's having a hard time – he wants to take his girl out, but his boss makes him work late; he wants to use the car but his parents won't let him. Finally he phones up his congressman, who, in a famous couplet says, 'I'd like to help you son, but you're too young to vote' leaving Eddie stuck with the Summertime Blues.

'C'mon Everybody', which followed, presented teenage situation No. 2. His parents have gone out for the evening so he calls all his friends down to party. The invitation is for everyone, and the song takes its place as a specifically teenage 'Rock Around The Clock'. You could imagine any number of bluesmen or R&B singers doing 'Rock Around The Clock', but who else could sing: "If my folks come home I'm afraid they're gonna tan my hide – there'll be no more movies for a week or two, no more hanging round with the usual crew" although, on the other hand....."who cares? – C'mon Everybody".

All-time classic that it was, 'C'mon Everybody' was too raw for 1959. Pop fans had gone soft, they didn't want to rock and they didn't accept Eddie's invitation to party. It never even made the Top 30. In Great Britain though, young people were still rocking and they sent the song straight into the Top 10. Cochran decided that it was time to cross the pond, and in 1960 he travelled to the British Isles.

Great Britain didn't have any rock'n'roll stars of its own at that time so the fans were hungry for the American masters. Eddie Cochran, like Gene Vincent with whom he toured, was seen as a great hero and he played to packed houses throughout the country. The tour was so successful that it was extended for another 10 weeks, but there was to be a short break between completing the old engagements and starting the new ones. Eddie and Gene decided to go home for a quick break. They hired a car and together with Cochran's fiancée Sharon Sheeley headed for London's Heathrow Airport. On the way there a tire blew and the car went skidding into a lamp post at 70 miles per hour. Vincent and Sheeley were hospitalized, Cochran was killed.

Eddie had a song in the charts at the time, and as the news of Cochran's death came in, it rose to number one. The name of the song? Everybody knows the name of that song. 'Three Steps To Heaven'.

ABOVE: *The writer of songs such as 'Teenage Heaven' and 'Teenage Cutie', Cochran had only just finished being a teenager himself when he died in 1960.*

1935
GENE VINCENT

1971

T he story of Gene Vincent is the story of mismanagement. He could have been a big star, but following the advice of his record company he was washed up before he even had time to establish himself.

Born in Norfolk, Virginia, Vincent left school at 16 to join the Navy. He might have stayed in the Navy were it not for a motorcycle accident he had while riding dispatch as part of his Naval duties. His left leg was severely injured, leaving him disabled for the rest of his life, but it was while he was recuperating from his accident that Gene turned seriously to music. In 1955, he began singing on Norfolk's country and western station WCMS. Station D.J. 'Sheriff' Tex Davis was impressed by Vincent, and arranged to record some demos with him which he then sent to Capitol Records. They were on the lookout for an Elvis clone, and offered Vincent a contract.

Gene went to Nashville with his band, the Bluecaps, and recorded 'Woman Love' and 'Be-Bop-A-Lula'. These cuts are the cream of rockabilly. They took the blueprint laid down by Elvis on Sun and made it their own. 'Be-Bop-A-Lula', cited by John Lennon as the most perfect of all rock'n'roll recordings, starts with Elvis' trademark 'We-e-e-e-ll' and jerks into three minutes of flawless music. Guitarist Cliff Gallup swoops in and out of Gene's vocal line, coming to the front to take two bang-on-the-nail solos.

Capitol were delighted with the results of the session and released the two songs within two weeks of receiving them. Although 'Woman Love' was billed as the A side, it was 'Be-Bop-A-Lula' that everyone started playing and it shot to the top of the charts. When two equally good rock-a-billy follow ups failed to hit the chart heights of 'Be-Bop-A-Lula', Capitol A&R man Ken Nelson tried to move Vincent away from rockabilly to a smoother sound calculated to appeal to a wider audience. In 1957 Elvis was scoring with songs like 'Let Me Be Your Teddy Bear'. Nelson, who had no great understanding of rock'n'roll, wanted Vincent to do likewise and leave the greasy Bluecaps behind. But Vincent was uneasy in the cute singer roll and just around the corner were real cute singers like Fabian and Ricky Nelson. It looked as though his career was already over.

By 1958 the Bluecaps had split, the tax man was after Gene and there were no more hits to bring the money in. He went to Great Britain where there was still a ready audience for hard rock'n'roll, and his live appearances in black leather earned him great popularity. He even notched

HIT RECORDINGS	
BE-BOP-A-LULA	1956
BLUEJEAN BOP	1956
LOTTA LOVIN'	1957

up a couple of hits there – 'My Heart' and 'Pistol Packin' Mama'. In 1960 Gene was touring with old buddy Eddie Cochran. They were driving to London's Heathrow airport when the car skidded into a lamppost, killing Cochran and injuring Vincent and Cochran's fiancée Sharon Sheeley.

When he had recovered from the accident, Vincent continued to tour, but by the time Beatlemania set in his audiences had thinned and he had started to drink heavily. He flitted back and forth between Great Britain and the United States hoping to rekindle his former fame, but was in no condition to reach his earlier heights. In 1971 he returned to California where a seizure caused by a bleeding ulcer resulted in his death on 12 October.

1936
BOBBY DARIN

1973

Bobby Darin is generally remembered for his dramatic and un-expected changes in musical direction. From rock'n'roller to folk singer, Darin took in the whole spectrum, including a spell as a big band singer and country musician, and even acquitted himself honour-ably as a songwriter, with songs like 'Dream Lover' and 'Splish Splash'.

Born to a poor family in the Bronx as Robert Walden Cassotto, he desperately wanted to be famous from an early age. He first hit on the idea of becoming an actor, and after choosing the name Darin from a phone book, he went on the road with an acting troupe. Soon, however, when it looked like acting was getting him nowhere, Bobby left acting and started writing songs. He was soon making contacts in the music business and his reputation as a songwriter was enough to convince Decca to sign him as a recording artist.

HIT RECORDINGS	
SPLISH SPLASH	1958
QUEEN OF THE HOP	1958
DREAM LOVER	1959
MACK THE KNIFE	1959
THINGS	1962
YOU'RE THE REASON I'M LIVING	1963
IF I WERE A CARPENTER	1966

LEFT: *Bobby Darin as an actor. Here playing a scene with Sidney Poitier in the film 'Pressure Point' (1962).*

LEFT: *Darin's youthful good looks ensured continuing support from women throughout his many changes of musical style.*

OPPOSITE TOP: *Bobby with wife Sandra Dee and son Dodd.*

OPPOSITE BELOW: *A role Darin always enjoyed was that of entertainer.*

Darin's partnership with Decca lasted through four flops before they dumped him. His next label Atlantic were about to do the same after similar disappointments when Darin talked his way into the boss' office and gave an impromptu performance of a new song that he said was sure to be a hit. Atlantic boss Ahmet Ertegun relented and gave Bobby an hour and a half of studio time to cut four sides. In that hour and a half Bobby recorded the number that was to make him: 'Splish Splash'.

'Splish Splash' made Darin a teen idol, and he quickly followed it up with 'Queen Of The Hop' and 'Dream Lover' – two other self-composed numbers that both hit big. But suddenly in 1959, Darin made his first change of direction. That he should have made it right then, at the peak of his success, is a matter of some surprise as a more cynical performer would have waited until he had milked his teen idol image for all it was worth before changing musical direction. As it was, Darin turned from a teen idol to an all-round entertainer overnight and only increased his success.

'Mack The Knife' was the song that announced the change in direction and it stayed at the top of the charts all autumn. It earned Darin a prestigious Grammy and built an unusual bridge across the generation gap. Record companies had always used the generation gap as a marketing ploy, believing that if parents didn't approve of the music then the kids would and vice versa. Darin had already hooked the kids and with this Sinatra-style number, he was now bringing in the adults too.

In 1960 Darin lived out his role as show biz celebrity – headlining at the Copacabana club, hosting a T.V. special and marrying actress Sandra Dee – and he was still only twenty-three years old. Where was he going to go from here? Taking a leaf from the book of both teen star Elvis Presley and adult star Frank Sinatra, Darin aimed for the movies. He had many lead parts without actually starring and he won an Oscar nomination for 'Captain Newman MD' in which he played alongside Gregory Peck and Tony Curtis.

But Darin didn't entirely give up music, in 1962 came 'Things' a country-style song that went Top 5 and then after signing to Capitol as a Frank Sinatra replacement he brought out a Ray Charles influenced song, 'You're The Reason I'm Living' which also made the Top 5. Thereafter his luck failed. There were four good reasons for this turn around in fortunes: John, Paul, George and Ringo. Bobby tried to draw on his adult support by returning to his earlier Sinatra-style material but when this too failed, he made the most startling transformation of his career and became a hippy. This wasn't just a pose, clean-cut Bobby Darin grew his hair, put on his jeans and went to live in a caravan in California. His music became meaningful, honest, socially aware.

When the hippy era was over Bobby moved back to the clubs. He was signed to Motown and sang the love theme in the company's film 'Lady Sings The Blues', but was stopped from making a comeback by bad health. His heart had been troubling him at the start of the 1970's and in 1971 he had two valves replaced. In 1973 he underwent another operation but didn't survive. He died at the age of 37.

RICK NELSON

HIT RECORDINGS	
1957	I'M WALKING
1957	BE BOP BABY
1958	STOOD UP
1958	WAINYIN' IN SCHOOL
1958	BELIEVE WHAT YOU SAY
1958	POOR LITTLE FOOL
1958	LONESOME TOWN
1958	I GOT A FEELING
1958	SOMEDAY
1959	IT'S LATE
1959	SWEETER THAN YOU
1959	JUST A LITTLE TOO MUCH
1961	TRAVELIN' MAN
1961	HELLO MARY LOU
1961	EVER LOVIN'
1962	YOUNG WORLD
1962	TEENAGE IDOL
1963	IT'S UP TO YOU
1964	FOR YOU
1972	GARDEN PARTY

The young Rick Nelson had no aspirations to being a singer, he fell into it by accident, but that accident yielded 53 Top 100 hits. An amazing feat when you consider that Buddy Holly had less than 10.

Hitmaking was something of a family tradition for the Nelsons. Rick's father Ozzie, had a dance band in the 1930's which clocked up 40 hit records between 1930 and 1940 and his mother Harriet sang with the band and had the distinction of introducing two Irving Berlin songs in the Astaire-Rogers film 'Follow the Fleet'.

In the 1940's Ozzie and Harriet had their own radio sit-com, 'The Adventures of Harriet and Ozzie', and it was here that Rick made his first appearances. On one show he appeared in, after the series had moved to television, the 16-year-old Ricky sang the Fats Domino hit 'I'm Walking'. He didn't sing it particularly well but his good looks carried it over and when Verve released it as a single, it went to No. 2 in the charts. From then on, singing took the place of acting.

Ricky's image was that of a watered-down Elvis, he kept the greased-back hair and faintly sneering smile, but anything provocative or truly rebellious was eliminated. Even the voice lacked any hint of Presleyesque threat. On the plus side, when he moved record companies to the West Coast Imperial label, he used material from the pens of Johnny and Dorsey Burnette, fellow Imperial artists who brought from Memphis a real rocka-billy feel. Then there was guitarist James Burton who played on all his records up to the mid sixties, reinforcing their rockabilly sound with classic solos. Burton was later to work with Elvis himself. Between 1957 and 1963 this winning combination gave Nelson an astonishing run of constant chart success, including such hit singles as 'Be Bop Baby', 'Stood Up' and 'Poor Little Fool'.

After the Beatles arrived in 1964 Rick, like the other artists who made their names in the rock'n'roll era, found himself cast aside. It took him a while to adjust, but towards the end of the 1960's he formed 'The Stone Canyon Band' which had in its ranks many members of the newly emerged country-rock scene; Randy Meisner, bass player from Poco and then The Eagles and Tom Brumley, steel player from Buck Owens band, for example.

In 1971 he appeared at a rock'n'roll revival show in Madison Square Gardens and performed his new country rock material. The crowd, expecting to hear all the old hits, booed him. In retaliation he wrote the song 'Garden

LEFT: *Even as a married man with a wife and child, Rick could not shake off the 'teen idol' image that his fans had forced on him.*

ABOVE: *Ricky appearing with Mother Harriet in the 1950's TV show 'The Adventures of Ozzie and Harriet'.*

Party' which explained how he had to go his own way, and notched up a surprise Top Ten hit with it.

'Garden Party' was to be his last hit, but Nelson continued to tour and it was on the way to a New Year's Eve gig in Iowa in 1985, that the plane he was travelling in crashed, killing himself, his fiancée and five others.

Rick Nelson was the most successful of the teen idols to come into prominence at the end of the 1950s, but if he was the marketing man's dream, he was also able to produce some enduring popular music over the years.

ROY ORBISON

1936

1988

HIT RECORDINGS	
1956	OOBY DOOBY
1960	ONLY THE LONELY
1960	BLUE ANGEL
1961	RUNNING SCARED
1961	CRYING
1962	DREAM BABY
1963	IN DREAMS
1963	MEAN WOMAN BLUES
1964	OH PRETTY WOMAN
1988	YOU GOT IT
1989	MYSTERY GIRL

Roy Orbison started performing at the same time as Buddy Holly, Jerry Lee Lewis and the Everly Brothers. He saw them all rise to stardom ahead of him, but after the rock'n'roll craze had died down and the others were finding it difficult to get work, Roy had the charts virtually all to himself and he stayed on top until the Beatles arrived with the British Invasion.

Roy was a quiet kid. He was studying at North Texas State University with a view to becoming a teacher, but was also playing in band, the 'Teen Kings'. When 'Ooby Dooby', a song written by two university friends, became a minor hit, it looked like it might be possible to earn a living from music, but Roy wasn't temperamentally suited to the wildness of rock'n'roll. He threw himself into it, affecting his own on-stage gyrations and snarlings but never felt at ease. The problem became worse when he signed to Sun Records and label boss Sam Phillips set about turning him into Elvis Presley mark two. Once again, Roy tried his best but all his recordings of that time sound wrong, forced. Roy's plaintive voice was meant for ballads, not for the rock'n'roll ditties he was given and, not surprisingly, none of them were successful.

Roy was beginning to wish he had taken his teacher's exams. He had married in 1956 and his wife Claudette was now pregnant. Sun had more or less dropped him after he'd been unable to get a hit and it looked like his short career was over. Then Phil Everly of the Everly brothers asked Roy if he had a song they could record as a B side to 'All I Have To Do Is Dream' and Roy played him 'Claudette'. This was to start the songwriting career that kept Roy afloat until he could come into his own in 1960.

RCA offered to record Orbison but Nashville manager Chet Atkins showed the same lack of sensitivity with Roy as Sam Phillips had done, foisting unsuitable and sometimes inferior material on him and then wondering why he wasn't successful. Roy left RCA for Monument where he was treated more sympathetically.

'Only The Lonely', released by Monument in 1960, was the sound of Roy. No longer was he imitating someone else or trying to sing how other people had told him to, this was the Roy's own sound and it was a sound people liked. His voice was high, inconsolably sad, but not false; the music was country and R&B, and the song co-written with friend Joe Melson. It got to No. 2 in the charts.

RIGHT: *Roy Orbison. His sunglasses were not a gimmick but a suggestion of a record company executive who felt that Orbison's eyes were too close together.*

The success of his sound, and of the songwriting team, persisted through another 12 hits, including such numbers as 'Running Scared', 'Crying' and 'Dream Baby', which were released up until 1964. His last big hit – 'Oh, Pretty Woman' came out the year the Beatles started their assault on the charts, and it made No. 1. The Beatles were to use the riff from 'Oh, Pretty Woman' in their single 'Daytripper' the following year.

Throughout these years of success, Roy's songs were generally melancholy; 'crying, lonely, running scared' and people wondered why. He was happily married, with three kids, and on top of the charts, there didn't seem to be a reason for Orbison's prevailing melancholia. But in 1966 he was given one. Wife Claudette was killed in a motorcycle crash and just two

ABOVE: *1987–88 saw a
revival of interest in Roy
Orbison. He recorded an
album with some of his
musician fans and was
inducted into the Rock 'n'
Roll Hall of Fame. This
photograph was taken at
his last ever concert at
Cleveland, Ohio on
December 4, 1988.*

years later, two of his sons were killed in a house fire. On top of all that, he
was going out of fashion and his records slowly stopped selling.

For 20 years, Orbison was in the wilderness, continuing to tour because
he had to, but appearing in smaller and grubbier venues. Pride would not
let him join the nostalgia bashes which periodically came up with has-been
stars of the 1950's, so he went his own way, doing shows around the world.
But in 1987 it looked like Roy was going to get another chance. Bruce
Springsteen had inducted him at the rock and roll Hall of Fame Ceremony
and went on to jam with him in a television spectacular in California.
Suddenly, everybody wanted to work with him. There was the 'Mystery Girl'
solo album that work began on the following year, and the 'Traveling
Wilburys' project with George Harrison, Bob Dylan and Tom Petty.

Busy throughout 1988, Orbison kept a high profile. He enjoyed working
on 'Mystery Girl' which included songs by Elvis Costello and Bono from
U2, and the single 'You Got It' gave Roy his first proper hit for more than 20
years. On 6 December, 1988 Roy was at his mother's house flying model
aeroplanes with a friend when he was suddenly stopped by a pain in his
chest. Later that night, his heart gave out. Although he is often thought of
as one of the original rock'n'rollers, Roy Orbison was never a rocker. His
time was later, in the early sixties when the high octane energy of rock'n'
roll had died down and people were looking for something smoother. But
there was no contrivance in his music, it was simply the product of a unique
imagination that fitted the times to perfection.

SAM COOKE

When people talk about 'sweet soul music', they don't mean sweet as in sugary, but a sweetness that combines beauty with pain. There is no better illustration of this than the singing of Sam Cooke.

Born in Clarksdale, Mississippi, Sam moved at an early age to Chicago where his father became a minister. There were numerous opportunities for the young boy to sing in church and when it was time to join a group it was no surprise that Sam joined a gospel group – The Highway QC's.

At that time gospel music was the hottest music around. It reached emotional heights that pop, blues or R&B could never hope to aspire to. Heaven, hell, indeed the whole universe was in question, and the emotions that this provoked stretched the musicians to the limits of expression. From these musical experiences, gospel vocalists evolved all the techniques that were later to form the basis for pop and soul singing, and the first singer to bring it into the pop world was Sam Cooke.

After leaving the Highway QC's, Sam joined one of the greatest of all the gospel quartets, the Soul Stirrers. Leading the group he had always looked up to, and taking the place of his idol Rebert Harris, was a daunting experience for Cooke, but gradually he gained in confidence and provided the Stirrers with a bonus in the form of his charm and good looks.

Whereas Rebert Harris had been able to whip up a crowd's religious emotions, the feelings that Sam was beginning to stir were not always 100 percent holy. The young people, who had always taken the back seats in the audience, soon moved up to the front, and the women, in the words of Wilson Pickett, 'fell like dominoes' when Sam began to sing.

By now Cooke had perfected the technique that would make him legendary. His singing was effortless, notes seemed to be suspended in mid air; his eyes would close and his arms raise up from the elbows as notes welled up within him and flowed out. Offers soon started arriving for Sam to sing for the secular world but he dismissed them out of hand; with gospel, he sang for the Lord; to sing just for money was akin to serving the devil.

But the offers continued to come, and Cooke began to wonder what would happen if he did release a pop song. To test the water, he released a gospel tune with lightweight pop lyrics, 'Lovable' under the pseudonym of Dale Cook. The name wasn't much of a disguise, and nor were the pop lyrics, Sam's voice was unmistakable and the gospel community was not pleased, they began to talk behind his back at the Soul Stirrers' concerts. Sam was

HIT RECORDINGS	
YOU SEND ME	1957
ONLY SIXTEEN	1958
WONDERFUL WORLD	1960
CHAIN GANG	1964
SHAKE	1964

unsure what to do, but when 'You Send Me' went to No. 1 on the national charts in 1957, Sam had his career mapped out for him. 'You Send Me', written by Cooke himself, didn't have the most complex lyrics in popular music – mostly it's just the title itself – but no one listened to the words, they were captivated by the voice, which had brought over from gospel all of its ethereal beauty. There was even the trademark 'Wo-oh-oh-oh-oh-oh-woh' linking verses.

Cooke now started getting interested in music publishing. He didn't want to be manipulated or trampled on like other singers who had been picked up by the music industry one moment and then unceremoniously dumped the next. He was already writing his own songs, so why not get the publishing rights as well? An old friend of his, J W Alexander, had just started a company of his own and Sam, with his newfound wealth and his songwriting ability, became a full partner. The two set up their own record company, SAR, recording in the first instance his ex-band the Soul Stirrers. Sam wrote and produced their first SAR recording, 'Stand By Me Father', which was to become the basis for the successful Ben E King song 'Stand By Me'. The label seemed to be used by Cooke as an outlet for expressing the side of himself that was suppressed by his pop songs. SAR artist Johnnie Morisette would record 'Meet Me at Mary's Place'; Sam would do 'Meet Me At The Twistin' Place'. It was a bit sad for fans of Cooke to see him releasing dance craze records like 'Everybody Likes To Cha-Cha-Cha' and 'Twistin' The Night Away', many of which he'd written himself. By this time the church had permanently disowned him and when he appeared with the Soul Stirrers during their anniversary concert, he was booed off the stage.

His writing deepened. Sam always gave the impression that he could turn his hand to anything; gospel songs, teenage ballads, dance songs; and now after hearing Bob Dylan's 'Blowin' In The Wind' he realized that he could write a serious song for the pop market. In 1964, 'A Change Is Gonna Come' was released; a mature and dark song, it seemed to prophesy the upsurge in black political consciousness that was to happen later in the decade. It was also the last of his records to be released while he was alive.

His death in 1964 seems sadly incongruous and melodramatic. Cooke met a young model at a party and offered to drive her home, but instead, he drove her to a motel and dragged her up to a bedroom. While Cooke was in the bathroom, she ran out, and when Sam discovered she'd gone he rushed down to the lobby, demanding that the night manageress tell him where the girl had gone. When she refused, Sam started to attack her; and she, in self defence, shot him dead.

To this day, many people refuse to believe this, saying that either he walked into the wrong motel and got someone else's bullets, or that it was all part of some white plot to get rid of the successful black businessman. A detective hired to examine the case though, could find no such evidence.

The unusual thing about Sam's voice was that it wasn't blatantly sexual like Elvis Presley's but rather that it seemed to inspire a pure kind of love from its listeners. There are many who feel that Cooke has no equal.

LEFT: *Sam Cooke's handsome appearance meant that not all of the women who packed out his gospel performances had their minds on spiritual things.*

1941
OTIS REDDING
1967

HIT RECORDINGS

1965	RESPECT
1965	I'VE BEEN LOVING YOU TOO LONG
1968	DOCK OF THE BAY

Otis Redding idolized singers Sam Cooke and Little Richard but when he came to sing he sounded like neither of them, he just sounded like Otis. He converted Stax of Memphis to his gutsy brand of soul music and gave the world a Southern alternative to the slick Motown sound.

Although he was born in Dawson, Georgia, he moved to Macon with his parents at the age of three. Macon already had two famous sons, James Brown and Little Richard, and it was seeing Little Richard live that started Otis thinking about music. It's hard to think of two people who are more unalike than Otis Redding and Little Richard but the gruff stomper began performing in the Little Richard style. By the time he came to make his first recording for Stax though, he was under the influence of Sam Cooke. He didn't go straight into the foot-stamping, horns-punching style that was later to be his own, but started on slow ballads like 'These Arms Of Mine' and 'Pain In My Heart'. 1965 was the year when the real Otis emerged and the song to proclaim his arrival was 'Respect'. Self-composed, this song contains all the features that came to be associated with the Stax sound. It starts off with bass and drums punching a note on each beat, followed by a tough riff from the horns. The bass frees from the beat, lays down a funky pattern against the fours and Otis comes in with his gruff call: 'What you want, baby you got it'. He'll give her anything and all he wants in return is some respect; as he says the word the horns come in to support his request. There were no backing singers at Stax, no shoo-be-doo's or doo-wops, just the hard riffing horns.

The Stax house band, the MGs, talk of how Otis energized them when he came into the studio, how he could bring everything together in a perfect blend; and it worked every time. Stax put out several albums like 'Otis Blue' and 'Dictionary Of Soul' which were recorded as albums rather than just being collections of singles. There were both Otis originals and covers, but Otis covers weren't copies but translations into his own style. Nothing could be further from Redding than Sam Cooke's 'Wonderful World' yet if you haven't heard the Cooke's version you'd swear it was an Otis original. Indeed this actually happened with the Rolling Stones 'Satisfaction' which many people thought the Stones had copied from Otis.

Word of the Stax sound spread, and when a revue toured Europe in 1967 the fans went crazy. Otis, the MGs, Eddie Floyd, Sam and Dave, and Otis

Otis Redding on stage. He could whip up a crowd into a frenzy of excitement with his foot stomping brand of southern soul.

protégé Arthur Conley were all amazed at the reception they got. The papers too were unanimous in their praise, Britain's New Musical Express proclaimed them 'the raviest, grooviest, slickest tour package that Britain has ever seen'.

Back in the United States, Otis was to work the same magic on the crowd at the Monterey Pop Festival. Rock fans who had come to see bands such as the Who and Jefferson Airplane suddenly found themselves listening to, and enjoying, straight Memphis soul.

Otis was now ready to breakthrough to the pop market. He had been the No. 1 man on the soul and R&B charts but had not yet scored on the pop charts. Now it looked like the goal was in sight. He began a determined series of gigs, flying from venue to venue in his private jet. One day in December 1967 he was advised against flying to a gig in Madison, Wisconsin — all commercial flights had been grounded due to adverse weather conditions, but Otis wasn't to be dissuaded. The plane crashed into a frozen lake just outside Madison killing him and several members of his band.

Ironically Otis posthumously achieved his aim as his last recording 'Dock Of The Bay' went to No. 1.

MARVIN GAYE

HIT RECORDINGS

1962	STUBBORN KIND OF FELLOW
1963	CAN I GET A WITNESS
1963	PRIDE AND JOY
1964	HOW SWEET IT IS
1965	I'LL BE DOGGONE
1965	AIN'T THAT PECULIAR
1968	I HEARD IT THROUGH THE GRAPEVINE
1969	TOO BUSY THINKING ABOUT MY BABY
1971	WHAT'S GOING ON
1971	MERCY MERCY ME
1971	INNER CITY BLUES
1973	LET'S GET IT ON
1977	GOT TO GIVE IT UP
1982	SEXUAL HEALING

WITH TAMMI TERRELL

1967	AIN'T NO MOUNTAIN HIGH ENOUGH
1967	YOUR PRECIOUS LOVE
1968	AIN'T NOTHING LIKE THE REAL THING
1968	YOU'RE ALL I NEED TO GET BY

One of the true artists of Motown, Marvin Gaye had always felt constrained by Motown's strict pop policy. When he finally broke out of it in 1982, he scored a worldwide smash with 'Sexual Healing' and the album 'Midnight Love'. Two years later he was shot dead by his father.

Music was not the sole interest of the young Marvin Gaye. Although he sang regularly in church his main ambition was to be an athlete but his father, a harsh Pentecostal minister, would not let him. To get away from both his father and the church, Marvin joined the Air Force at the age of 17. Although he liked the flying, he was not so keen on military discipline and was soon discharged.

Marvin then turned seriously to music. He sang with a succession of doo-wop groups, and in 1959 joined the Moonglows – one of the most famous of all doo-wop bands. Marvin and Moonglows' leader Harvey Fuqua met the future Motown boss Berry Gordy in Detroit, who asked them to join his new organization, and both Marvin and Fuqua went on to marry Gordy sisters – Marvin marrying Anna and Fuqua, Gwen.

Motown at that time has often been described as 'a family' and Marvin was definitely family, but he didn't get star treatment from the word go, as some disgruntled Motown employees have alleged. He started off as a session man, playing drums on many records, including some by Smokey Robinson and The Miracles. For his own career, he envisaged himself as a jazz/pop singer like Frank Sinatra or Nat King Cole and persuaded Gordy to record him in that manner. Gordy allowed him three singles in this style, but when they all flopped, he decided on a change in pace.

Martha Reeves and two other Motown employees were summoned to add spice to Marvin's next release 'Stubborn Kind Of Fellow', and they added so much spice that Marvin gave them the name 'Vandellas' kidding them that they had vandalized the session. But the funky move away from jazz gave Marvin his first hit and set the standard for a series of up-tempo numbers that followed. In 1964, he paid back the Vandellas by co-writing their summer smash 'Dancing In The Street' and embarked on a series of duets with Motown's top ladies.

His first musical partner was the then current Queen of Motown, Mary Wells, but she only made one record with Marvin, after which her boyfriend persuaded her that Motown was ripping her off and she could do much

LEFT: *Marvin Gaye singing in 1964. On his face, a mixture of puzzlement and joy.*

better elsewhere. He negotiated a contract for her with Twentieth Century Fox under whose tender care she was swiftly consigned to oblivion. Marvin, meanwhile, had a few solo hits, including 'How Sweet It Is To Be Loved By You' and 'Aint That Peculiar'. Mary Weston became his next partner and she stayed for one hit before history repeated itself and Mary, too, left Motown to improve her career but was never heard of again.

ABOVE: *Marvin with Tammy Terrell. They recorded a series of definitive boy/girl classics.*

The last partnership had a more painful end. Tammi Terrell with whom Marvin cut such definitive boy/girl classics as 'Aint No Mountain High Enough' and 'Aint Nothing Like The Real Thing', collapsed on stage in Marvin's arms. Tammi Terrell had a brain tumour and despite many operations, died in 1970. This affected Marvin so much that he couldn't perform for nearly four years after that, but he had already notched up his biggest hit two years earlier with 'I Heard It Through The Grapevine'.

The death of Tammi Terrell left Marvin in an angry mood. He wasn't going to be pushed around by Motown, and decided to take control of his career, writing songs about real subjects and producing the next album himself. Motown executives laughed at the results, as 'What's Going On' contained songs about poverty and the ecology, subjects that had never come up on any other Motown records but somehow Gaye managed to persuade the company to release the album and it spawned three Top 10 hits: 'Mercy Mercy Me', 'Inner City Blues' and the title track 'What's Going On'.

Buoyed on by his success, Gaye now released another album 'Let's Get It On', centred around another subject never openly tackled at Motown – sex. Sex to Marvin Gaye was not something outrageous or naughty as it was to other pop stars, but something natural and divine. His unique approach must have struck a refreshing chord as the single 'Let's Get It On' went to No. 1 in 1973.

He'd been serious on one album, sensual on the other, Marvin seemed to have expressed all he wanted to express and he was determined not to go back to being a Motown puppet. But it wasn't Motown that made him record his next album, it was demanded by court order. When he divorced Anna Gordy in 1978, he was asked to make two albums and to sign over all the royalties to her. The title of the resulting double album – 'Here My Dear' is typical of the contents; it is clearly a record made under duress, and it's not too hard to work out who the barbed attacks that crop up in the songs are aimed at.

Marvin now entered a low period. He had been forced to do 'Here My Dear' because he had declared himself bankrupt before divorce proceedings began and now he was just as poor and in a foul mood. Driven away by tax men and creditors he ran to Hawaii and London, his paranoia increased by large amounts of cocaine. Then suddenly in 1982 came 'Midnight Love' with its perfect single, 'Sexual Healing'. Marvin Gaye had come back and was restored to the top of his profession. 'Sexual Healing' was as natural and unforced a number as could be and summed up the very essence of the man.

For all those who were looking forward to more music from the back-on-form singer, news of his death came as a shock. Perhaps it was fitting that his last hit was so perfect, as it was his last. During a heated argument with Gaye Senior, the Pentecostal preacher ran out of words and replied instead with bullets, shooting his son dead on 1 April, 1984.

1944
DENNIS WILSON

1983

Dennis was the middle of the three Wilson boys. Brian, the eldest, had all the attention of a first born child and Carl, the youngest, was the baby of the family, so Dennis then became the hellraiser. When they became the Beach Boys later, Brian was the eccentric genius, Carl, the lovable, quiet one and Dennis remained the hellraiser.

The first Wilsons to sing together were Brian, Carl and parents Murray and Audree. Dennis rebelled and would not join in, but when Brian wanted to form a group without father Murray, Dennis was interested. He even suggested they write a song about his latest passion – surfing.

The brothers first sang at a talent show at school before auditioning for a recording and publishing company. When they were told that they needed something special to stand out from the crowd, Dennis mentioned the group's song 'Surfin'. The record executive liked the song and offered to record it. The song was a minor hit, but Dennis did not actually play on it. He had argued with the rest of the group and was kicked out; Brian played drums on the record.

Audree Wilson was not pleased to hear of Dennis' eviction and made sure he was reinstated. With Murray Wilson managing the group – now called the 'Beach Boys' they got a deal with Capitol Records in 1962 and hastily began writing surfing songs. Over the next three years, the group meticulously exploited every aspect of surfing life: 'Surfing USA', 'Surfer Girl', 'Girls On the Beach', 'Don't Back Down' – all because of Dennis' fondness for the sport.

On tour, the muscular, blond Dennis was a great hit with the girls. This caused friction with his cousin and fellow Beach Boy Mike Love, who was rapidly growing bald and resented Dennis' position as 'sex symbol' of the group. The rock'n'roll lifestyle appealed to Dennis, the drinks, drugs, reckless spending, and even though he'd married in 1965, the groupies. He spent money freely, but not always on himself, if he saw anyone in need he'd step in and help. His first wife Carol remembers coming home once to find the washing machine and drier gone. When she confronted Dennis, he explained how he'd met a man who had five kids but who'd lost his job, so he gave him the washing machine and drier to help. He and Carol later divorced.

This soft side of Dennis nearly got him into trouble in 1968 when he came home to find an unexpected house guest. Cult leader Charles Manson

HIT RECORDINGS WITH BEACH BOYS

SURFIN' USA	1963
SURFER GIRL	1963
LITTLE DEUCE COUPE	1964
FUN FUN FUN	1964
I GET AROUND	1964
WHEN I GROW UP TO BE A MAN	1964
DANCE DANCE DANCE	1964
HELP ME RHONDA	1965
CALIFORNIA GIRLS	1965
BARBARA ANN	1966
SLOOP JOHN B.	1966
WOULDN'T IT BE NICE	1966
GOD ONLY KNOWS	1966
GOOD VIBRATIONS	1966

RIGHT: *Of The Beach Boys, only Dennis was interested in surfing. And it is he, more than anyone else who was responsible for their surfing, cars, girls and fun image.*

OPPOSITE: *The Beach Boys. With Chubby Carl, balding Mike Love and Al Jardine, Dennis Wilson (centre) was the heart throb of the Beach Boys.*

had moved in with his 'family' of 12 young girls and Dennis walked into the house to see some of the girls topless, smoking pot and listening to the hi-fi. Manson appeared a bit sinister and had some funny ideas, Dennis felt that anyone who could simultaneously attract 12 good-looking girls whose devotion to him was complete had to be something. Manson rationalized his drugs and orgies lifestyle with philosophy, and Dennis was hooked.

Dennis allowed Manson to take over the house to the extent that Manson ordered the girls to go through Dennis' wardrobe and cut up all his clothes into squares. Then they were to sew all the squares into robes. Dennis wasn't angry when he found all his clothes had been cut up, but went along with it happily, wearing his multicoloured robe. More dangerous was when Dennis began promoting Manson as a musician of genius. He finally convinced friend Terry Melcher to help Manson with his musical career but Melcher was soon put off by Manson's psychotic behaviour and didn't want anything to do with him. It was this that apparently led to the savage murder of actress Sharon Tate and five others at Melcher's old home in mid 1969. Manson wanted to frighten Melcher because he'd lost interest in him.

Dennis, meanwhile was on tour with the Beach Boys, but until Manson was caught, he lived in perpetual fear of him. Manson had already called at Dennis' new house and left a bullet from his gun with the message 'This is for Dennis'. Things were going badly for the Beach Boys in general, as

ABOVE: *The Beach Boys in the film 'Girls on the Beach' (1964). Although the group only appeared in a musical capacity, in this film, Dennis was later to appear in the cult movie 'Two-Lane Blacktop' (1971) in an acting role.*

residing genius Brian was unpredictable, the magic evaporated from the music without him. By the hip, turned-on late 1960's, the Beach Boys seemed like a relic from another era.

In the seventies Dennis went into decline, smashing rental cars, getting drunk, one time even smashing a plate glass window with his fist which stopped him from playing drums for a year. His rivalry with Mike Love continued and when Dennis beat him up on stage he was barred from touring for two years. He started going to psychotherapy and friends were surprised to see him keep it up for many weeks. They later discovered that the psychotherapist was a beautiful woman and Dennis was trying to get her into bed.

In 1983 he spent a considerable amount of time around Marina Del Ray, on the Southern California coast. On one occasion after he'd been drinking heavily, he decided to go diving to recover effects from an old boat of his that had sunk there. He came up to have some sandwiches then went down again. This time he never resurfaced.

1942
JIMI HENDRIX
1970

HIT RECORDINGS	
HEY JOE	1967
PURPLE HAZE	1967
THE WIND CRIES MARY	1967
ALL ALONG THE WATCHTOWER	1968
VOODOO CHILE	1970

J imi Hendrix was a true musical talent. What Elvis Presley was to the voice, Hendrix was to the guitar. They both had the ability to draw on a power outside themselves and channel it through their instruments and with Hendrix the effect was increased still more by his use of electricity – he amplified what was already electric and astonished the world.

Jimi Hendrix was born in Seattle, Washington and was given his first guitar while at school. He took to it immediately, and when word got round that he could play he noticed a change in his classmates – particularly the girls. Those who had previously ignored him, now started to take an interest. This was a foretaste of things to come.

After doing his military service, Jimi Hendrix worked professionally as a guitarist backing such artists as B. B. King, Jackie Wilson, Sam Cooke and the Isley Brothers. He was earning a living but had no room to express himself behind such strong frontmen. His break came in 1966 when Animals bass player Chas Chandler saw him playing in a New York club. Chandler was so impressed with what he saw that he instantly gave up his own career as a musician to become Jimi's manager. They both flew to

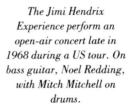

The Jimi Hendrix Experience perform an open-air concert late in 1968 during a US tour. On bass guitar, Noel Redding, with Mitch Mitchell on drums.

London where Chandler had contacts in the rock world who he felt sure would be as impressed with Hendrix as he was. He got bass player Noel Redding and drummer Mitch Mitchell together and the three musicians began to perform in the clubs as the Jimi Hendrix Experience.

In the 1960's Great Britain had become the unlikely home of the blues. Hundreds of youngsters up and down the country followed the example of the Rolling Stones and formed blues bands. Some of these bands were better than others, but in general they came out like pale imitations of their Chicago mentors. When Hendrix hit Britain an original had arrived, and everyone knew it.

The first people to rave about Hendrix were the musicians: Eric Clapton, Pete Townshend, Paul McCartney, Jeff Beck and others flipped, and Hendrix began moving in the hippest inner circles of swinging London. The press also quickly latched on to Hendrix, and in addition to his music they had Hendrix's onstage activities to write about. He played the guitar with his teeth, he stabbed at it with his crotch, he played it behind his head, he banged it against the amp and in a final mad frenzy, smashed it up completely. This, combined with the music, made watching Jimi live an unbeatable experience. Hendrix conquered London, then Great Britain, then Europe. The only place left to conquer was the United States.

The immediate occasion of Hendrix's return to the US was the Monterey Pop Festival of 1967. Paul McCartney had told the selection committee for the festival that Hendrix was 'a musical pioneer, a creative genius' and that they had to book him. They did, and America fell for the gifted maniac.

1968 was a peak year. After Monterey he had become a superstar, commanding capacity crowds wherever he played, his albums were going gold and praise was coming from all quarters. Even tight-lipped jazz trumpeter Miles Davis spoke out and hailed him as a genius. Hendrix now plunged headlong into the rock'n'roll lifestyle, endless tours, all-night parties, drugs, groupies, so that by the beginning of 1969 he was a tired man.

But there were other problems too. His audience was 90 percent white, and the Black Power movement felt that Jimi should be doing something towards improving the situation for black people worldwide. After all, no other black musician had ever attained such a high position in rock music before. Bob Dylan had shown how music could be used to promote social ideas, and yet Hendrix was singing about nothing but love and peace. He was obviously not going to start writing political songs, but when inner tensions split his white band, he took advantage of the situation by forming a new band with two black musicians hoping to appease those campaigning for Black Rights.

The new group, the 'Band of Gypsies' did not last, however. During their second, and last, concert at Madison Square Gardens, Jimi had an attack of 'bad vibes'. They were performing on a revolving stage which was annoying Jimi, he broke a string, tried to recover but eventually walked off the stage and never returned.

Then there were legal problems. When Chas Chandler whisked Hendrix

away to London he didn't realize that Jimi was already under contract to manager Ed Chalpin in New York. All this time he had been in breach of contract and legal proceedings had already been started against him. Without the guiding hand of Chas Chandler, who had gone in 1968, having found it impossible to get anything done when all those around him were either tripped out or stoned, Jimi was at sea. To add to Jimi's troubles, there was a court case hanging over his head all year stemming from an incident at Toronto Airport where a bottle containing heroin was discovered in his flight bag. Jimi made no secret of the fact that he took many drugs, but heroin was definitely not one of them. He told the court that a woman had given him the bottle when he complained of stomach ache, and he put it in his bag, believing it to be Bromoseltzer. There was a witness who testified that she saw the whole event and Jimi was acquitted on 11 December, 1969.

The Isle of Wight Festival in England in 1970, proved to be his last concert. He gave a fine and restrained performance but there were no guitar bashing theatrics, it was just the music. Back in London, he threw himself into a relentless round of parties. He returned one night to his girlfriend's flat after having drunk a lot, had a meal, then took some sleeping pills and went to bed. The lethal combination of drink and pills caused him to choke on his vomit while still unconscious; he never woke up.

Jimi Hendrix blazed brightly for three brief years, but packed more raw musical energy in those three years than most musicians manage in their entire lives. The guitarist's spot in rock'n'roll heaven is forever Jimi's.

1943
JANIS JOPLIN

1970

HIT RECORDINGS
1968	PIECE OF MY HEART
1971	ME AND BOBBY McGEE

Angry, sad, anguished – when Janis Joplin sang the blues she was more than just blue. Her unhappy childhood in Port Arthur, Texas, was to leave a permanent scar on her life and influence on her music. She was shy, vulnerable and intelligent but never fitted in with other girls at her school, who mercilessly made fun of her. They picked on her for her short stumpy build and bad complexion, making her the butt of endless jokes, and while she tried to laugh with them their constant rejection led her to seek the company of a small group of boys, drinking, swearing and acting as they did. Inevitably, the new, tough tomboy Janis was despised even more by her classmates and by Port Arthur in general, their implacable dislike creating an almost pathological need to be loved in Janis.

When she started at the University of Texas at Austin, Janis looked forward to meeting a more intelligent group of friends and being accepted for herself. She needn't have bothered. She was nominated by the students for the 'Ugliest Man on Campus' award and with that she left university, left Texas and headed for San Francisco.

When Janis arrived in 1963, San Francisco was beginning to emerge as the hippie capital of the world. If there was anywhere she was going to feel at home, it was here. She started to sing the blues, using it as a form of emotional outlet. While English blues bands would sing lyrics a million miles away from their own experience, Janis sang her words with a deadly seriousness intent. She started off as a soloist, but her unusual and powerful sound quickly attracted the attention of rough and ready blues rockers 'Big Brother And The Holding Company' who asked her to front them.

To hear 'Big Brother' with Janis was an experience indeed. She bawled, she wailed, sounds that had never come out of a singer's mouth before came out of hers. All the pain she had suffered, all the hurt she had felt poured out in a torrential flood. The effect was overwhelming. In June 1967 Joplin appeared at the Monterey Festival and the laid-back, flower-toting crowd, were shaken to the core by the aural onslaught delivered by her and the band. She attracted the attention of everyone; the crowd, who almost matched the power of the band with the intensity of their applause; Albert Grossman, Bob Dylan's manager who quickly became Janis'; and the press, who considered her a new sensation.

What delighted the press more than the music itself was the Joplin image. She projected herself as a boozy, man-eating goodtime gal who

ABOVE: *Janis in happier times.*

54

LEFT: *Although she could put on a tough exterior, Janis could never quite hide her child-like vulnerability.*

RIGHT: *The period of Janis' greatest success coincided with the age of the pop festival. She appeared both at Monterey and Woodstock.*

BELOW: *On a diet of drink, drugs and free sex, Janis became an archetype of the late 1960s rock star.*

didn't care what she said or did as long as she was having a good time. Maybe she thought that if she really threw herself into it she would forget all the hurt and actually begin to enjoy herself, but there was more than a touch of desperation about the way she did it. Truly happy times were very rare for Janis – as a friend put it, 'even when she was happy she was unhappy'.

After recording the album 'Cheap Thrills' with Big Brother, new manager Albert Grossman suggested she start working as a solo artist. 'Cheap Thrills' did succeed in capturing the spirit of the band but it also magnified the lack of discipline of their playing. Janis, though, emerged as as a startling and original talent. In 'Ball And Chain' and 'Piece Of My Heart' she made

angry, desperate appeals for love such as had never been heard before on record. At the end of 1968 she left Big Brother, taking guitarist Sam Andrews with her to form a new band.

Janis' status as a star steadily increased, as did her reputation as a reckless hedonist. She boasted of hundreds of sexual encounters with men, many of them true, drank almost constantly and started using heroin. Her self-destructive streak seemed to make her want to punish herself: when told that her drunken behaviour could get her into trouble she replied that it served her right for being so ugly.

Despite this constant abuse, it was a sad irony that Joplin's fatal heroin overdose came at one of the happiest times for her. She was in love with Seth Morgan, a student at Berkeley University who seemed to return her feelings, and they were making plans to marry. She was also finishing the last few tracks of an album with which she seemed very pleased. There is no doubt that her overdose was accidental, it was caused by the exceptional purity of the heroin combined with the low tolerance she had developed over several months before, when she had been off the drug.

Ever since her schooldays in Port Arthur, Janis Joplin had been a tortured soul. She tried to cover up her immense unhappiness with her brash good-time gal act, but whenever the mask fell, she looked heartbreakingly vul-nerable. If some people said that her anguished screams weren't singing they were right, it wasn't just singing songs with her, it was pure emotional exorcism.

JIM MORRISON

1943

1971

HIT RECORDINGS WITH THE DOORS

1967	LIGHT MY FIRE
1967	PEOPLE ARE STRANGE
1968	HELLO, I LOVE YOU
1969	TOUCH ME
1971	LOVE HER MADLY
1971	RIDERS ON THE STORM

Jim Morrison, one of rock music's most unruly children, came from a conventional middle-class family with a long tradition of serving in the armed services. His father was a Naval officer and Jim was brought up in the comfortable Florida town of Melbourne.

He graduated from George Washington High School in 1961 and went on to Florida State University. In 1964 he moved to Los Angeles and studied theatre arts at UCLA. It was here that he met the future Doors keyboard player Ray Manzarek. Ray had always been interested in music and Jim was interested in poetry, he read Ray some verse he had written and Ray was amazed, he suggested they form a group at once, Jim agreed and thought of a name for the band from a poem by William Blake "If the doors of perception were cleansed/All would appear infinite". They were to be the Doors.

The Doors started playing gigs in 1965 and because they didn't have that much material, they extended songs, going into improvisations while Jim recited his poetry. 'The End' which began as a short song about lost love, ended up as a number in which Morrison expressed a wish to kill his father and sleep with his mother. Audiences of the time were shocked to hear Jim shouting 'Father I want to kill you, Mother I want to...(he screams) and the first time the Doors performed it like this at the 'Whiskey A Go Go' they were kicked out.

Word of the Doors spread and soon they were recording for Elektra. The surprising thing about this most outrageous of groups was the fact that they had two No. 1 hits — 'Light My Fire' and 'Hello, I Love You'. Other West Coast 'underground' bands like the Grateful Dead never even made it into the charts.

Jim's stage act was also something apart. He came on stage in a pair of skin-tight, leather trousers and writhed about as if in sexual ecstasy. After surprising everyone with his Oedipus routine in 'The End' there was always the feeling that Jim was going to do something wild. Crowds watched with fear and anticipation almost willing him to go over the top. He certainly wasn't a conventional singer, in fact he never thought of himself as one at all and if the band were playing a number that no longer interested him, he would sing a few lines and then drop out.

When Morrison began appearing on stage drunk or under the influence of drugs in 1968, it really was anybody's guess what he would do. One time he

fell off the stage, on another he stopped singing altogether and began to tell a series of unfunny jokes. But the most notorious occasion was the one of April 1969 in Miami where he allegedly exposed himself on stage. The band members have alternately admitted and denied that this was done, but according to Ray Manzarek interviewed in 1981: "Jim said to the audience, 'That's enough, you didn't come here to hear music… you came here for something you've never seen before, something greater and bigger than you've ever experienced…how about if I show you my cock?" He then began dancing around with his shirt over his groin, lifting it just once to give the audience a lightning flash.

After the concert a warrant was issued for Jim's arrest, and he retreated to Paris. Sick of being a rock star and being hounded by the press and police, he grew a beard, put on weight and became almost unrecognizable. He had just finished recording the album 'L.A. Woman' with the Doors and they were all pleased with the results. The album was strong, containing the classic track 'Riders On The Storm' and the band waited for Jim to return from Paris to begin work on a new album. But Jim never returned.

Some people continue to doubt the death of Jim Morrison. They point to the suspicious circumstances surrounding his death; the sealed coffin, the illegible certificate giving heart attack as the cause of the death, and the lack of witnesses following the death of his wife Pam in 1975. Supporters of the theory claim that Jim was trying to get away from it all — that he might have faced a jail sentence after the incident in Miami, so he faked his own death. One of Morrison's heroes was the French poet Arthur Rimbaud who gave up poetry at 19 and wandered around the world incognito; some fans say that Morrison might have done the same. While he was with the Doors, though, there is no doubt that Jim Morrison took music, particularly live music, into unchartered realms. He really did break down the doors of what could or could not be done.

BRIAN JONES

HIT RECORDINGS WITH ROLLING STONES

1964	TIME IS ON MY SIDE
1965	THE LAST TIME
1965	I CAN'T GET NO (SATISFACTION)
1965	GET OFF MY CLOUD
1966	19TH NERVOUS BREAKDOWN
1966	PAINT IT BLACK
1966	LET'S SPEND THE NIGHT TOGETHER
1968	JUMPING JACK FLASH

Intelligent, well spoken, Brian Jones was born into a comfortable family in Cheltenham, England, on 28 February, 1942. He was the first of the Rolling Stones to start going down to the Ealing Blues Club where many of the British bluesmen of the 1960's served their apprenticeships. Members of the Animals, Kinks, John Mayall's Bluesbreakers and Cream all spent time jamming here with the house band, Blues Incorporated.

When Mick Jagger and Keith Richards walked into the club, they saw Jones up on stage doing what they had dreamed of doing – playing the blues. Jones befriended them although some of the older club members looked down on them for playing Chuck Berry numbers. Brian, though, saw his future was with Jagger and Richards so he formed a band with them, calling it the Rolling Stones after a Muddy Waters song.

Brian acted as the manager of the group. When they started playing together, Mick was studying at the London School of Economics and Keith was at art school. Only Brian with his eyes on the Beatles, thought of the Stones as a possible career. He was relentless in getting bookings for the band and successfully got them a residency at the 'Crawdaddy' club in Richmond's Station Hotel not far from London.

The Crawdaddy gigs showcased the raw appeal of the Stones. Their delivery of American originals was straight and suffered from none of the 'sweetening up' that usually occurred when white musicians covered black material. The music was undeniably exciting, with a harder edge than more commercial rock'n'roll. The Stones capitalized on their rawness and were determined to hold on to it when they hit the big time.

In the audience of one of the Crawdaddy gigs was Beatles press officer Andrew Loog Oldham. He saw the Stones as rebels and realized that they could carve out a niche for themselves playing the bad boys against the Beatles' lovable moptops image. Oldham was 19 and talked the same language as the Stones, but as he moved in to execute his masterplan, Brian was getting slowly edged out of his position as leader. To make matters worse, Jagger, as the singer, was attracting all the attention. Jones' ambivalent attitude to Mick Jagger meant that when a powerful booking agent agreed to give the Stones some work on the condition that they 'get a better singer', Jones quite happily agreed. Fortunately, Andrew Loog Oldham did not agree.

A fatter, puffy-eyed Jones. The Rock 'n' Roll lifestyle was beginning to take its toll on him.

Oldham was successful in getting over the image of the Stones as anti-authority figures. He encouraged them to be rude, to let their hair outgrow the Beatles' and get in the news as often as possible for disreputable acts such as being thrown out of restaurants for not wearing ties. This publicity play began to irk Jones who resented being called dirty and a moron.

If Oldham had usurped Brian's managing role, Mick and Keith were beginning to take over as band leaders. Mick, of course, standing up front, petulant and arrogant, commanded all the attention, and when Jagger and Richards started to write their own material, they cemented the bond between them that excluded Jones. He found himself playing a less and less important role, and frustration turned him to the faithful rock'n'roll stand-bys of drink, drugs and groupies.

When the Stones became targets for drug raids in the late 1960's, Brian, as the heaviest consumer, was the most vulnerable. Throughout 1967 he would be arrested, allowed out on probation, arrested again, released and then arrested once more – in the words of Jagger, it was this 'continual harassment' which finished Brian off. The Stones' bad boys image inevitably pulled them into trouble. The Beatles, perceived as good guys and loved by the press, were making statements about how LSD had changed their lives but were not busted until much later.

To get away from it all, Jones, Richards and Jones' girlfriend Anita Pallenberg, went for a trip to Morocco in 1968. Pallenberg, an aristocratic Italian model, was a status symbol for Brian but when his temper flared and he started to beat her, Richards drove her home to safety. By the time Jones got back to England, Pallenberg had switched allegiance from Jones to Richards. Jones was angry and took less and less interest in the group. He started to miss sessions and when he did turn up he was frequently too drugged or drunk to contribute. The Stones carried on without him.

Finally, in 1969 he left the band with the statement. 'I no longer see eye to eye with the others over the discs we are cutting'. Although this would have been understandable in 1967, when the Stones were going through their psychedelic phase, by 1968 they had made a triumphant return to the blues, releasing the classic 'Jumping Jack Flash' and the album 'Beggars Banquet', which many regard as their best. So what was the truth behind Jones' departure from the band?

He had been fired by the others. They knew how important he had been to the band in the past, but now he was unreliable, confirming everyone's worst ideas about the Stones.

Jones put on a brave face about the sacking, pretending that he didn't care, but he was devastated. He retreated to his new country home in Cotchford, a house previously owned by A A Milne, author of 'Winnie The Pooh'. Here, terrified of being busted again, he allowed no drugs into the house and turned instead to drink. It was after a considerable drinking bout that he decided to go for a night swim in his swimming pool. He was found lying face down at the bottom of the pool. It was just one month since he'd left the Rolling Stones.

JOHN LENNON

1940

1980

HIT RECORDINGS

969	GIVE PEACE A CHANCE
970	INSTANT KARMA
970	POWER TO THE PEOPLE
971	IMAGINE
972	HAPPY XMAS (WAR IS OVER)
981	JUST LIKE STARTING OVER
981	WOMAN

John Lennon brought many unexpected things to the role of pop singer. Intelligent, witty, scathing and irreverent, he was the one that gave the Beatles their edge and endeared them to intellectuals and others who wouldn't normally have bothered with pop music.

Soon after his birth in Liverpool in 1940, John's parents drifted apart. His father, a merchant seaman sailed away, never to be seen again until John was famous; and his mother, Julia, handed the infant over to her more responsible sister Mimi. Lennon quickly proved himself to be leader of the gang at school. His magnetism and strength drew people to him in admiration and fear. His first main interest was books, and in particular 'Alice In Wonderland' and 'Alice Through The Looking Glass' but as the 1950's rolled on he discovered rock'n'roll. He strongly identified with the energy, aggression and rebellion of the new music and wanted to form a rock'n'roll band straight away.

Jonn's great hero at this time was Elvis Presley and as a teenager John Lennon actually was what Elvis appeared to be: a true rebel. There was no 'sir'ing' and 'ma'aming' for Lennon, he respected no one unless he felt they specifically deserved it. Age or social rank did not impress him, even when the Beatles had become famous, John could still come out with a scathing comment like the one he made to the audience at a Royal Variety performance: "For the next number would the people in the cheap seats clap your hands? And the rest of you rattle your jewellery."

While still at school, Lennon formed 'The Quarreymen' and at one of their first performances in 1955, he met a young, chubby Paul McCartney. Paul impressed him, knowing all the words to the Eddie Cochran song 'Twenty Flight Rock', and by playing the guitar far better than John, who immediately asked him into the band. Apart from their love of rock'n'roll, they also shared an interest in song writing, and spurred each other on to great heights of invention.

When John was 18 his mother, Julia, was run over by a car. Julia had just started coming back into John's life at this point and from all accounts she had quite a similar character to his. She was wild, anarchic, she would go out with a pair of long knickers on her head, which earned the singular approval of John. Furthermore, she was musical and taught him how to play the guitar. When she died Lennon showed no outward sign of emotion but began to display a more cruel streak. Friends remember walking with him

WITH THE BEATLES

SHE LOVES YOU	1963
I WANT TO HOLD YOUR HAND	1964
CAN'T BUY ME LOVE	1964
TWIST AND SHOUT	1964
A HARD DAY'S NIGHT	1964
I FEEL FINE	1964
EIGHT DAYS A WEEK	1965
TICKET TO RIDE	1965
HELP	1965
YESTERDAY	1965
WE CAN WORK IT OUT	1966
NOWHERE MAN	1966
PAPERBACK WRITER	1966
PENNY LANE	1967
ALL YOU NEED IS LOVE	1967
HELLO GOODBYE	1967
LADY MADONNA	1968
HEY JUDE	1968
GET BACK	1969
COME TOGETHER	1969
LET IT BE	1970
LONG AND WINDING ROAD	1970

ABOVE: *The Beatles live in 1964. Years of performing in tough Hamburg clubs had turned the Beatles into a tight, efficient, four piece group.*

past crippled or deformed people and hearing Lennon say in a loud voice 'Some people will do anything to get out of the army'.

After school he enrolled at the Liverpool School of Art because, as he put it, it was better than working. He had fought his way through school and now he turned up at Art College in his leather jacket, tight 'drainpipe' trousers, looking as if he'd start a fight with anyone who so much as looked at him. His future wife Cynthia, who he met there, admitted later that at first she was frightened of him but the two started dating and later in 1962 when Cynthia became pregnant, they married.

The Quarreymen meanwhile, had turned into the 'Silver Beatles' and got themselves club bookings in the West German city of Hamburg. Away from home and parental interference, John found himself free to do as he liked. His first action on his arrival in Germany was to shoplift a mouth organ. He insulted the patrons of the 'Star Club' at length, knowing that they couldn't understand English, and led a pig on a lead through the streets of Hamburg's red light district, the Reeperbahn. On the other hand, he posted his weekly earnings home to Cynthia in England and wrote her love letters with comments on the envelope such as 'Postman, postman, don't be slow, I'm in love with Cyn so go man go'. He could be warm as well as nasty.

It was largely John that attracted manager Brian Epstein to the Beatles. Epstein was certainly no rock'n'roll fan, but he was fascinated by the rebellious arrogance of Lennon. Beatles music was state-of-the-art pop music. Lennon and McCartney had built on the pop legacy of rock'n'roll, Goffin and King, Phil Spector and even Motown to come up with a pop style that would please everyone. But a large part of their enormous success was due to their off-beat humour. With Paul and Brian Epstein in charge, they might have been conventional entertainers, but with John leading the way, they seemed witty, frank and funny. When asked to account for the success of the Beatles, John simply replied, 'We have a press agent'.

By 1965 the Beatles had conquered the world. They had become media darlings, and more importantly had the musical ability to sustain their reputation. Each record was an advance on the last – they weren't writing to public taste, they were creating public taste and all notions of what a pop group should be like were cast aside. Paul would come out with an orchestra, George with a sitar, no one could predict what they would do next but each time they amazed the world.

In 1964 came Lennon's entry into the literary world. 'In His Own Write' was a collection of short pieces that showed Lennon to be an original, confident and hilarious writer. It was a worthy addition to the tradition of English 'nonsense' writing, even if some of the pieces exhibited a cruelty that would have given the author of 'Alice in Wonderland' a fit.

John's honesty finally got him into trouble in 1966 when he claimed that the Beatles were more popular than Jesus. When this comment was printed as a headline in magazine 'Dateline' it caused a furore. Everyone who had a grudge against the Beatles but who couldn't, up until then, find anything to attack them for, were suddenly given a gift – heresy. What John had actually said wasn't shocking at all and when Brian Epstein asked him what

RIGHT: *The Beatles had earned so much money for Britain that in 1965 they were awarded M.B.E.'s (Member of the Order of the British Empire), which led many other members to send back theirs. John got in on the act himself in 1969 by returning his M.B.E. in protest against Britain's support of American involvement in Vietnam, and 'Cold Turkey' slipping in the charts.*

ABOVE: *From 1962–1965 The Beatles changed little in appearance. From 1966–1970 they seemed to change every week. Here, they model the Moustachio look.*

should be done, John's remark was 'Tell them to get stuffed'. In order to appease the public and press though, he apologized, but thousands of Beatles fans, spurred on by right-wing groups had already set about burning Beatles records and paraphernalia.

1967 saw some serious dream weaving from Lennon. Gone were the simple 'I Love You Girl' songs of before and in their place, tangerine trees and marmalade skies, Kings and Duchesses and Henry the Horse dancing the waltz. It was the land of nursery rhymes and fantasy – nothing could be further from traditional rock'n'roll than 'I Am The Walrus'. Some people put this change in writing down to LSD, a drug that Lennon had first sampled in 1966, but it is entirely possible that all these songs could have been written under the influence of Lewis Carroll. At this time John really was in a world of his own. While Paul was hanging out with the trendy London art scene, John was at home in suburbia with a wife and kid –'sitting in an English garden waiting for the sun'.

Then he met Yoko. It is hard to think of a woman who had a more powerful effect on her man than Yoko Ono. Her ideas were to completely dominate John Lennon over the years ahead. Before, Lennon had always been the independent one – people followed him but he followed no one, now it seemed that he was completely under the spell of Yoko. He changed his middle name from Winston to Ono and even seemed to want to look like her, shaving off his moustache and growing his hair long like hers.

They began to record together. 'Two Virgins' was an album of noises – screams from Yoko and birdsong, but its real importance lay in the cover. A photograph showed John and Yoko completely naked facing the world. Yoko's values were somewhat different from those of the Beatles.

John divorced Cynthia and, after marrying Yoko, the couple appeared before the Viennese press in a bag. The other Beatles were disconcerted when John's outside activities impinged on theirs like when John started to bring Yoko to rehearsals – in a bed. She didn't do much for the solidarity of the band and when the Beatles broke up, John formed a band called the 'Plastic Ono Band'. At first Yoko contributed ear-splitting shrieks to the music but then wisely left the vocals to John. She wasn't going to let him sing love songs though. His first album with the 'Plastic Ono Band' was about John's mother Julia and he bared his soul to an unprecedented degree on 11 tracks including the succinct 'My Mummy's Dead'. The production was sparse, the singing anguished, it was hardly easy listening.

The next album 'Imagine', produced by Phil Spector, was more pleasant sounding but the title track – the most famous of all Lennon solo songs – was practically a communist manifesto. No countries, no possessions, no religion, no heaven. Yoko had discovered that the latest thing was radical politics and over the next two years she dragged John on a blind political trip round all the current political causes – for feminism John wrote 'Woman Is The Nigger Of The World', for Ireland 'Sunday Bloody Sunday' and 'The Luck Of The Irish'. John was hounded by the CIA for his activism, but quickly tired of politics preferring the dream world of the poet to the gritty realism of a politician.

The 1970's seemed a period of retirement for John. He seemed to lose interest in music, his few recordings were half-hearted efforts, and finally in 1975 they stopped altogether. He explained this break from musical activity as an opportunity to raise his son with Yoko, Sean. He finally came out of retirement in 1980 with the album 'Double Fantasy' which featured Yoko on half the songs. He began to give interviews again and seemed a more sane, mature but still witty and intelligent person. At the end of 1980, a Beatles fan called Mark Chapman asked for John's autograph. John gave it. The following day John returned home from the recording studio with Yoko. They got out of the car and started to walk towards the doorway. A voice called out 'Mr Lennon', and as John turned round, Chapman fired five bullets into his back. He died on the way to hospital from loss of blood.

No one knows what drove Chapman to shoot Lennon. He didn't seem to have a reason. Some say he was just mad, others that he had been brainwashed by the CIA, whatever the reason, the grief that followed John's death was genuine and global. This wasn't just another rock'n'roll death, this was a Beatle death; the dream really was over.

John and Yoko, together for over 20 years. She was with him when he was shot in December 1980.

1949

KEITH MOON

1978

**HIT RECORDINGS
WITH THE WHO**

1965	I CAN'T EXPLAIN
1965	ANYWAY, ANYHOW ANYWHERE
1965	MY GENERATION
1966	SUBSTITUTE

They called him 'Moon the Loon' and for once, the nickname was accurate. Moon lived out his image to the full and eventually paid for it with his life.

Keith was a Beach Boys fan, playing with a band called 'The Beach-combers' when he turned up one night to see the Who. They were outrageous, frightening even, but nonetheless Keith asked them if he could sit in. They agreed, and he proceeded to lash into the kit so forcefully that he broke the bass pedal and two skins. Afterwards, Pete Townshend came up to him and with the words 'What are you doing next Monday?' invited Moon into the band.

The Who were a power pop band and Moon was definitely a power drummer, he slotted right into the machinery of the Who. There was guitarist Townshend with his angry, slashing chords, John Entwistle, solid on bass, and then Moon on percussion following the other instruments, punctuating phrases, jumping into the frontline and pushing the whole band forward as well. With this unbeatable combination, the Who were to overtake the Kinks as premier Mod band.

The Who had their finest moment with the single 'My Generation'. A savage track, Moon is relentless in propelling it on from the drums with a full kit including two bass drums and numerous toms. The verses of the song have lines that are delivered by Roger Daltrey which are then answered by the band – 'People try to put us down...' (band come in) '...Just because we get around....'(Band come in again), and Moon cannot wait to jump in. At one point, Daltrey is holding things up with his st..st..st..stuttered delivery so Moon unleashes a ferocious roll that overwhelms Daltrey, pulls the band back in and seems to say 'Come on Roger, stop hamming it up'.

Off stage, Moon was the man responsible for instigating the hotel room-smashing routine that was to become a trademark of rock bands on tour. But he also loved playing practical jokes – attaching invisible wires to Jim Capaldi's drum kit, so that as he played, part of his kit magically rose in front of his eyes; or dressing up as a vicar and arranging to be kidnapped in full view of two policemen who went after him in a manic car chase. The vicar gear was not the only outfit Moon had. He loved dressing up, and would often act out the part of the perfect English gentleman; a female seductress; a German chauffeur; or one of many other roles that he always played to the full.

LEFT: *Moon with a youthful looking Who, already challenging the camera.*

ABOVE: *Moon in a turn of the century swimming costume. Dressing up was a great love of his.*

ABOVE: *Moon performing with The Who in the mid to late 1960s. Beneath all the maniac clowning, Moon was rock's finest drummer.*

Moon had secretly married in 1966 and turned the family home into a 24 hour party zone. By 1974, his wife Kim had had enough and she left him. At this time, the Who had been together for 10 years and had done it all – they led the Mods, they had chart success, they had gone into rock operas with 'Tommy' and 'Quadrophenia' and now they had all gone their separate ways recording solo albums.

Moon moved to Los Angeles where he indulged in drinking battles with rock stalwarts Ringo Starr and Harry Nilsson, and made a disastrous solo album. He returned to Great Britain in 1978 an ageing, pudgy and tired man and his death later that year surprised no one. It was predictably a drug overdose, but ironically the drug was a specially prescribed one Moon was taking to help overcome his alcoholism.

Moon is remembered as the first virtuoso drummer in rock. He was the one who drew attention to the drums by playing in a way that forced itself to be listened to. Even jazz drummers like Buddy Rich had a good word for Moon, because in a world where rock drummers are either functional or flash, Moon contrived to be musical.

1946
DUANE ALLMAN

1971

In the 1960's no British rock group was complete without a 'guitar hero'. Guitar heroes like Eric Clapton, Jeff Beck and Jimmy Page seemed to be a purely English phenomenon until the arrival of two Americans: one was Jimi Hendrix, the other Duane Allman.

Duane was born in Tennessee in 1946 but after his father's death, the family moved to Florida's Daytona Beach. From the early 1960's, Duane and his brother Gregg started to play in youth clubs, performing a mixture of R&B and blues, and in 1963 they formed the 'Allman Joys'.

After a move to Los Angeles, the brothers became part of the band 'Hour Glass' and recorded two albums with them. Duane, however, was never satisfied with these albums, feeling that he was creatively stifled and forced to play things against his will. He returned to Florida and began to build up a reputation as a session musician, playing at the Fame Studios, Muscle Shoals, behind such artists as Wilson Pickett, Boz Scaggs, Aretha Franklin and King Curtis. But his ambition remained to run his own outfit, and after signing with Otis Redding's manager Phil Walden, he put together 'The Allman Brothers'.

The Allman Brothers drew on a rich mix of Southern influences – traditional blues, gospel, R&B and country, adding an authenticity that was missing in their British blues revivalist counterparts. The band had a two guitar front, with Duane playing slide and Dickie Betts riffing patterns behind him. The band became the group of the South – the West Coast had the Grateful Dead, the South had the Allmans.

Although the band were steadily building up a following, Duane was still doing sessions for other musicians like Otis Rush, Delaney and Bonnie and most notably Eric Clapton. Duane Allman and Eric Clapton trading riffs on the album 'Layla' marked a high point in both of their careers.

The motorcycle accident that resulted in his death came at the peak of Duane's achievement and success. He was riding down Macon Street, Georgia when a tractor trailer pulled out in front of him. He crashed trying to avoid the vehicle and died hours later on the operating table.

Although the Allman Brothers continued after Duane's death, they had lost his leadership and eventually, lost direction. At the time of Duane's death, however, the Allman Brothers were an influential band who set the pattern for a whole series of Southern bands like Lynyrd Skynyrd and the Marshall Tucker Band.

ABOVE AND LEFT: *From Mop-Tops to Weird Beards. The Allman Brothers were the U.S. answer to the British led blues boom of the 1960s.*

BOB MARLEY

1945

1981

HIT RECORDINGS	
NO WOMAN NO CRY	1975
EXODUS	1977
JAMMING	1977
IS THIS LOVE	1978
COULD YOU BE LOVED	1980
BUFFALO SOLDIER	1983

No music was more natural than the music of Bob Marley. Almost every other musician has succumbed at one time or another to marketing, hype or commercial pressures, but Bob Marley stayed solid. His music was simple, clear and flowed out of him as easily as breathing.

Although the Kingston, Jamaica ghetto Trenchtown featured largely in his songs, Bob Marley was actually born in the country town of St Anne. His mother, Cedella Booker was a poor farm worker and his father, Norval Sinclair Marley, was an English army officer from a rich family. Norval's parents disapproved of his alliance with Cedella and threatened to cut him off financially if he didn't leave her. He did.

To keep her family, Cedella had to work so they moved to Trenchtown close to Kingston where jobs were plentiful. It was here that he met Bunny Livingstone and Peter Tosh and formed the 'Wailin' Wailers'. From the start the group was different. Even as teenagers, the Wailers were concerned about poverty and social injustice. Their very first single 'Simmer Down' was an appeal to rival gangs in Trenchtown to cease their fighting. At the time of its release in 1963, other songs dealt with dancing, love and cars, but the Wailers were already singing for peace.

The Wailers sound changed as rhythms evolved in Jamaica, but they always had a distinctive vocal sound, with Bob singing lead beneath the high soaring harmonies of Bunny and Tosh. They got their inspiration for this from the US vocal groups of the 1950's like the Moonglows and the Impressions. The Wailers were successful in Jamaica throughout the 1960's, but due to the workings of the Jamaican record industry, very little money actually reached them. Bob realized that the only way they could improve their position financially was by having international hits but he didn't know how this was to be done.

In fact, it was being done for him. A white Jamaican, Chris Blackwell had set up Island Records in London to distribute Jamaican records in Great Britain. He had already had success in popularizing the music locally, but was looking for someone to make it big internationally. He gave the Wailers time and money and asked them to record an album for him. The result – 'Catch A Fire' established the group in Britain.

To support the record, the Wailers began to tour but this soon affected Bunny's health. He was homesick as it was, and wanted to return to

ABOVE: *Bob Marley –
reggae's ambassador to the
world.*

Jamaica. When the Wailer's second album 'Burning' was released under the name of 'Bob Marley and the Wailers' Bunny and Tosh both left the band, leaving Bob to carry the torchlight by himself. The two ex-Wailers had written songs for the group but there was no doubt that Marley was the main man. Retaining the name Bob Marley and the Wailers, he replaced Bunny and Tosh with three women vocalists and carried on as if nothing had happened.

The music continued, same as before, each album containing a selection of new songs and reworked numbers from the 1960's. The sound was unique and appealed to a worldwide audience: lilting slow reggae rhythms, throbbing bass and Bob's lyrics drawn from the Bible and Rasta lore. Never had preaching sounded so attractive – and meaningful.

In 1976 there was an assassination attempt on Marley at his Kingston home when gunmen burst in and sprayed shots around the room. Bob got a bullet through his arm, but it was his manager Don Taylor, who was between the gunmen and Marley, who took most of the shots. Miraculously though, he survived. Many theories have been advanced as to who was behind the assassination attempt; some say politicians were involved, others that Don Taylor was the real target and he'd got in trouble with his gambling; or perhaps it was related to Marley's scandalous affair with Miss World Cindy Brakespeare. Whatever the motive, shootings were not uncommon in Jamaica – ex partner Peter Tosh was shot 10 years later when burglars broke into his home. Marley's calls for peace were not empty mouthings.

When Marley hurt his toe playing football in 1977, medical treatment revealed a cancerous growth on the injured toe and Bob was advised to have the toe amputated. Instead he chose to have minor surgery and rely on herbal cures.

The album 'Exodus' recorded in London in 1976 contained three songs about the shooting – 'Guiltiness', 'Heathen' and 'So Much Things To Say'. Yet the B side of the album consisted of a suite of love songs that showed the lyrical side of Marley to the full. Jamming became a Top 10 hit in Great Britain, and the album also provided 'Wait in Vain' and 'One Love'. Marley was not possessive about his songs: if a friend was in need, Marley would credit the song to him thus ensuring them a continual source of earning in royalties.

In 1979 he wrote a song called 'Zimbabwe' about the state of Rhodesia, and all his militant feelings and ideas of freedom from oppression came into sharp focus. 'Every man got the right to decide his own destiny' came the no-nonsense first line, and when Zimbabwe did finally achieve independence from British rule later that year, Bob was asked to come over and play the song at the independence ceremony.

The next year, Bob continued to travel, taking on an extensive world tour that started in West Africa and ended in New York. After one of the New York concerts he collapsed with what doctors at first attributed to exhaustion. Closer investigation however, revealed that the cancer that had started

in Marley's toe had spread throughout his whole body. Doctors in New York told him nothing could be done to save his life, but Bob wouldn't accept this and he headed for the Josef Issels Clinic in Bavaria. He lost his locks under the chemo-therapy but seemed to be making a recovery. Tragically, the recovery was only temporary and he decided to go home to Jamaica for the short time that remained to him. He died on 11 May, 1981 in Miami on his way home.

Marley's contribution to musical history lies not just in the music he made, but also his lyrics of defiance and spirituality. The political and spiritual idealism of the 1960's had all but disappeared by the 1970's but Bob Marley continued to express such sentiments in his work right up to his death in 1981.

ABOVE: *One of the things that made Marley stand out from his contemporaries was his great gift for song-writing. He wrote political songs, love songs and spiritual songs, all with the easy assurance of a true master.*

1942
HARRY CHAPIN
1981

HIT RECORDINGS

1974 CAT'S IN THE CRADLE

Before settling permanently on a musical career, Harry Chapin was a pilot in the Air Force, had worked as a film editor, directed a documentary that was nominated for an Oscar and also wrote music for the underwater shark movie 'Blue Water, White Death'.

Chapin was born into a musical household in Greenwich Village, New York. His father Jim was a swing drummer who'd played in the bands of Tommy Dorsey and Woody Herman, and his brothers Tom and Steve played in various bands and also released solo albums. Harry's first public appearance was with the Brooklyn Heights Boy's Choir, and by 1964 he joined his father and brothers in a group that played round the Greenwich Village clubs. The group made an album 'The Chapin Brothers' but split up when Tom and Steve returned to school.

Harry also went into full-time education, first at the Air Force academy where he trained to be a pilot, and then at Cornell where he studied philosophy. After college, Harry went into movies, progressing from gopher to film editor to director, and his documentary on boxing 'Legendary Champions' was nominated for an Oscar. It was while writing music for another movie, that Harry began to think seriously about a career in music. He had already written several songs for an album his brothers made and now he wanted a crack at it himself. Steve got a band together, Harry wrote some songs, and they rented out 'The Village Gate' in New York where they started to give concerts. The move paid off, and Harry was recommended to Elektra Records who signed him up to a contract.

Unlike other singer-songwriters of the era – Joni Mitchell, James Taylor and others, Harry's songs were not self confessional, they rarely even involved himself at all. He would spin out stories over the verses or write from the point of view of a character, which made a refreshing change to the constant soul searchings that were common at that time.

His first album for Elektra, 'Heads And Tails' was released in 1971 to great acclaim, and it contained the hit single 'Taxi'. A successful run of albums and singles followed: 'Short Stories' of 1973 was a collection of narrative tales including 'W.O.L.D.' – a song about an ageing D.J. and 'Verities And Balderdash' of 1974 contained 'Cat's In The Cradle'. This song – about a father who has no time for his children – may have been a bit sentimental for some tastes, but it was simple and it struck a chord, making its way to No. 1 on the pop charts.

A prolific artist, Chapin kept up a steady pace of one album a year even though his sales fell off after 1975. Chapin involved himself in other projects, one of which was a musical revue called 'The Night That Made Hollywood Famous', an experimental show mounted on Broadway which was nominated for two Tony awards by the New York Theatre critics. His Hollywood review 'Chapin' highlighted his concern for world poverty and hunger, and he also organized several benefit gigs for various charities.

By the time of his death in a car crash in 1981 he was out of fashion, but his talent was unique and he did leave a void. Furthermore, his charitable acts – and it's estimated that he averaged about 100 benefit gigs a year – made him the one-man 'Live Aid' of the seventies.

1943
JIM CROCE
1973

HIT RECORDINGS

1972 YOU DON'T MESS AROUND WITH JIM

1972 OPERATOR

1972 BAD BAD LEROY BROWN

1972 I GOT A NAME

1973 TIME IN A BOTTLE

J im Croce must be one the unluckiest pop stars ever to have existed. His long struggle to get a record contract came to nothing when he failed to have a hit; and having worked as a lorry driver for four years to support himself and his wife, he was allowed just one year of success following his arrival in 1972 before he was killed in a plane crash.

Jim, born in Philadelphia, Pennsylvania, was playing the accordion at the age of six. He later attended the University of Villanova where he had a radio show and played in various bands, and left college set on a musical career. Working a variety of manual jobs by day, he and his wife Ingrid performed in coffee houses and bars by night. After four years of making themselves known around the clubs, the couple were noticed by Capitol Records who signed them up to make the suitably titled album 'Jim And Ingrid Croce'. When it flopped, however, Capitol dumped the Croces.

Jim went back to driving trucks and during the four years that followed, he developed his simple direct, everyday style of songwriting. While other young musicians had been snapped up by the music business in their late teens, Jim had full experience of life before he was given his next chance at the age of 28. As a songwriter it was valuable experience for him and while others pontificated about life, Jim seemed like a breath of fresh air.

In 1971 he submitted a collection of his songs to the New York production team Terry Cashman and Tommy West. West was an old college friend of Croce's and both he and Cashman liked the songs. They went ahead with the album 'You Don't Mess With Jim', a collection that conjured up the world of bars and car washes, striking a chord with the public who put the title single into the Top 10.

Suddenly Jim was in demand. 'Operator', also taken off the album as a single continued his success, and he rushed into the studio to record more. 'Life And Times' which came out in 1973, was an even greater triumph, giving Jim a No. 1 hit with 'Bad Bad Leroy Brown' and it seemed as if Croce with Cashman and West, had struck gold. The music had a wide appeal; folk audiences liked its acoustic sound; pop audiences enjoyed the catchy melodies; and rock fans related to its real life evocations.

The next and last album, 'I Got A Name' was finished in 1973 but Jim wasn't to see its release. He was killed with his guitarist Muary Muehleisen in an airplane crash in Louisiana at the peak of his success. 'Time In A Bottle', a single from the album, went to No. 1 as soon as it was released.

OPPOSITE: *Jim Croce performing live on 'Midnight Special'. His songs were not drug induced fantasies, but simple tales, set in the real world.*

78

1947

MARC BOLAN

1977

HIT RECORDINGS

1970	RIDE A WHITE SWAN
1971	HOT LOVE
1971	GET IT ON (BANG A GONG)
1972	TELEGRAM SAM
1973	20TH CENTURY BOY

Marc Bolan is remembered by those who knew him as a small mischievous imp who charmed his way to the top. Behind his mischievous image though, there was determination and Bolan was successful – in Great Britain at least – in achieving his goal of becoming a big star.

He was born in London's East End just after the end of World War Two. His father was a lorry driver and his mother ran a stall in a street market. The young Marc showed a particular interest in two things – rock'n'roll music and clothes. His interest in fashion and his youthful good looks led him to become a child model, an experience which left him with an enduring love of being on the spotlight. When he taught himself the guitar in his early teens he had found a way to stay in the spotlight while also pursuing his love of music.

One day in 1966 he marched into music manager Simon Napier-Bell's office with his guitar on his back. He told the astonished Napier-Bell that he was going to be a great star, and that he needed a good manager to look after the business side of things; Brian Epstein was too middle class, he said, and Rolling Stones manager Andrew Loog Oldham was too camp. He then started to run through some songs. After about ten songs Napier-Bell stopped Bolan and booked some time in a local studio. They drove over together and taped the whole lot.

Bolan's voice was totally original. Napier-Bell knew pop inside out but had never heard anything like it: high, with an idiosyncratic vibrato, it came over with a confidence bordering on arrogance. The songs themselves were just as original, catchy, and strewn through with Bolan's quirky, poetic word play.

Knocked out by the music, Napier-Bell was also charmed into submission by the Bolan personality. The fledgling pop idol regaled the manager with poetically exaggerated accounts of his life. It wasn't that he was telling lies about his past, but rather that his imagination turned even the most mundane events into magical experiences.

At the time, Napier-Bell was managing a band known as 'John's Children', and when their guitarist left he put Bolan in. But Bolan, the great individual, could never be happy submerged in a group and soon left. Without a band or even his guitar, he decided to forsake the electric world and form an acoustic band. When he heard of a drummer called Steve Peregrine Took,

BELOW: *Marc Bolan enjoying himself on stage at the height of his fame in the early 1970s.*

OPPOSITE: *Capes, satin and silks: Bolan believed in dressing up for his audiences.*

80

Bolan recruited him – more for the sound of his name than his percussive abilities – and formed Tyrannosaurus Rex.

With only acoustic guitar and bongos behind him, Marc indulged his romantic imagination for fairies, elves and magic. The title of his first album, 'My People Were Fair and Had Sky In Their Hair But Now They're Content To Wear Stars On Their Brows' showed Bolan was in a world of his own. No one could understand what he was singing about – even the song titles didn't make sense – 'Salamanda Palaganda', 'Trelawny Lawn' and 'Aznageel The Mage'. Then suddenly, the other-worldly elf would hit out with a straight ahead rocker like 'Mustang Ford' or 'Hot Rod Mama'. Even in fairyland Bolan had to bop. The mix was intriguing and delivered with such a sense of purpose that it soon attracted a dedicated cult following.

Some people thought that the Bolan's fantastical imagination was triggered off by drugs, particularly LSD, but although he had tried the drug in 1969, it had been an unpleasant experience and one that he would never repeat.

From 1968 to the end of 1970 Marc enjoyed the status of being a cult figure but still wanted the greater glory of stardom. He had named his band deliberately: Tyrannosaurus Rex was the biggest mammal ever to have existed on earth; Bolan was going to be the biggest star. When one of his catchy, up-tempo numbers 'Ride A White Swan' was released as a single in 1970 it caught on. Bolan's dream came true.

BELOW: The star at home. Bolan had been a child model and was used to having his photograph taken.

In 1970 stars were thin on the ground. It was a time when musicians considered themselves to be artists rather than mere entertainers. They would offer their music but that was all – no dressing up, no posing, just the music. Bolan changed all that. He didn't just want people to listen to his music, he wanted people to look at him. In Great Britain, a whole generation followed in Bolan's steps, pouting and posing, made up to the eyeballs and with stardust in their hair. These were the 'Pretty Things' David Bowie was to sing about and Marc had started it all.

The first people to respond to Bolan's new pop image were teenage girls. They reacted with a fervour that had not been seen since the time of the Beatles. These teen and pre-teen girls took control over the British charts and kept Bolan on top for the next two years.

Success soon took its toll on Bolan. The pixie side of his nature began to get submerged beneath his ambition. He began to talk of marketing, distribution, sales figures and gross receipts. He became filled with his own importance, failing to credit people who helped him and alienating old friends like disc jockey John Peel. It was Peel who had got Bolan noticed by continually playing his records and supporting his group. When he remarked that he didn't like one of Bolan's records, the singer ended their friendship there and then, never speaking to him again. Musically, Bolan had got stuck in a groove. In his early days he was literally bursting with ideas, but now he was having hits with boogie songs; he would only release numbers in the same style. He soon ran out of variations.

More worrying still was his failure to duplicate his British success in the United States. Rod Stewart had made it there, so had Elton John; so why not Marc? He tried, but his fey brand of rock'n'roll seemed to be too effete for the country where rock'n'roll was invented. He returned to England dispirited and told everyone that he had been a knockout hit.

Meanwhile, his teenybopper fans were fast growing up and getting real boyfriends. Time was running out and by 1975 he was finished. Failure was something that Bolan could never accept. In his last years he talked of his lack of success as a 'retirement', and spoke of the bad effects of fame, as if he was deliberately releasing poor records in order to avoid being famous again.

In 1977 Marc Bolan seemed a more mature person. He had his own television show and used it to give exposure to some of the emergent punk rock bands like The Damned and Generation X. It seemed as though his enormous craving for fame and attention had subsided. Then on September 16, while riding in a mini with his girlfriend Gloria Jones, the car swerved off the road and went into a tree, killing Bolan and injuring her.

Years before, Simon Napier-Bell had told him that if he wanted to be successful and to own a Porsche like James Dean then he should listen to some advice. 'Oh no', said Marc, 'A Porsche wouldn't be right for me, I'm too small. I think a mini is the right car for me. If I was going to die in a car crash, it ought to be in a mini'. If his life hadn't gone exactly to plan, at least his death had.

ABOVE TOP: *Marc with bongo player Steve Peregrine Took, his partner from 1967–1969 in the cult duo Tyrannosaurus Rex.*

ABOVE: *On stage with the electric incarnation of T-Rex, Marc became the first glam-rock superstar.*

ANDY GIBB

HIT RECORDINGS

1978 I JUST WANT YOUR EVERYTHING

1978 (LOVE IS) THICKER THAN WATER

1979 SHADOW DANCING

A ndy Gibb was five years old when his brothers Barry, Robin and Maurice had their first hit in Australia as the Bee Gees in 1963. Soon afterwards, the family moved back to England, their native home, and Andy went to school there. He suffered from being treated differently to other children because of his famous musical brothers, a situation that wasn't helped by being chauffeur-driven to school every day in a Rolls Royce.

At 13, his family moved again, this time to Spain, and it was here that Andy first started playing and singing. He was encouraged by his brothers, who bought him his first guitar, and in 1973 there was talk of him joining the Bee Gees although nothing came of it. But by 1976 Andy had started writing songs, and after putting together a tape of them, he was signed to Bee Gees record company RSO. If RSO thought they were doing Barry, Robin and Maurice a favour by signing the 19 year old, they were soon to find Andy just as potent a hit maker as his brothers.

In 1977-78 the world was Gibb mad. The Bee Gees had started the disco boom, having written the music for 'Saturday Night Fever' and embarked on a series of six unbroken No. 1 hits. How could Andy possibly make an impression with all this going on? His first album, 'Flowing Rivers' was produced by Barry who also contributed backing vocals. The first single released from it, 'I Just Want To Be Your Everything', in true Gibbs Brothers-style went to No. 1. The next single, '(Love Is) Thicker Than Water' did the same and the title track of his next album 'Shadow Dancing' gave the youngest Gibb his third consecutive No. 1.

At 19 Andy had become a star, but having started his career off so well could now only go into decline. He acquired a cocaine problem, splitting up with his girlfriend Victoria Principal largely because of it and made no new recordings.

At the start of the 1980s Andy made a career move into theatre. He appeared on Broadway in such productions as 'Joseph and the Amazing Technicoloured Dreamcoat' and the Gilbert and Sulivan opera 'Pirates of Penzance'. Although he had taken drugs in his time, his death in Oxford, England in 1988 was not a drug death. He had gone to the famous Betty Ford clinic in 1985 and was said to have left the clinic cured of any drug problem. The official cause of his death was attributed to a viral infection of the heart.

LEFT: *Andy Gibb – the fourth of the hit-making Gibb brothers. Between 1978 and 1979 he chased his brothers up and down the pop charts. He managed three No. 1's while they had four.*

ABOVE: *Andy with his parents in NYC. The family had been in music before Barry, Robin and Maurice formed The Bee Gees, father Hugh had been a bandleader in Britain.*

19??
LYNYRD SKYNYRD
1977

HIT RECORDINGS
1974	SWEET HOME ALABAMA
1974	FREE BIRD

R onnie Van Zant, Gary Rossington and Allen Collins were school kids together at Jacksonville High in Florida. Their first passion was Pop Warner baseball and it was only when Rossington saw The Rolling Stones that he convinced the others to form a band.

The young band went through a number of name changes before settling on 'Lynyrd Skynyrd'. The name came from a teacher, Leonard Skinner who had expelled the band for having long hair, although he did later make up with the group and even introduced them at one of their gigs.

In 1972, after adding Ed King to their guitar pool of Rossington and Collins, they attracted the attention of musician Al Kooper, who signed them to his new 'Sounds Of The South' label. Kooper produced their first album 'Pronounced Leh-nerd Skin-nerd' which included a 10 minute tribute to Duane Allman's 'Freebird', one of the most memorable of the band's tracks. Following the release of the album, their first major tour was as support to The Who. Playing stadiums and arenas was quite a change from the Southern bars and clubs they were used to and the band would often go out on stage to face 20,000 Who fans. They came out of it very well though, impressing fans and getting a big career boost.

Their second album 'Second Helping' contained 'Sweet Home Alabama' their answer to Neil Young's anti-redneck song 'Southern Man'. The Lynyrd Skynyrd song became a surprise Top 10 for them.

The first accidents to involve Lynyrd Skynyrd members happened on Labor Day weekend in 1976. Both Gary Rossington and Allen Collins were involved in separate car crashes: Allen had been drinking and went into the back of a parked car; Rossington fell asleep at the wheel and went into a telegraph pole, a tree and a house, causing over $7,000 in damage. Ronnie Van Zant wasn't very pleased with his reckless band mates and wrote 'Oh That Smell' warning them about the dangers of mixing 'whisky bottles and brand new cars' and 'too much coke and too much smoke'.

On their next album 'Gimme Back My Bullets' producer Tom Dowd added three backing singers and one of them, Cassie Gaines had a brother Steve who was to replace Ed King when King left in 1976. With the new line up Lynyrd Skynyrd went back on the road and recorded the live album 'One From The Road' in Atlanta, Georgia. Performing in front of the Confederate flag, with Ronnie in bare feet and three guitarists with their heads down riffing, the band had never been in better form.

But it was heavy touring that led to the tragedy of 20 October, 1977. The band had taken off from Greenville, South Carolina, in their private jet en-route for Baton Rouge, Louisiana when the plane came down in woods outside Gillsburg, Mississippi. Ronnie Van Zant and Steve and Cassie Gaines were all killed. MCA immediately recalled the band's album 'Street Survivors' whose cover showed the group standing amidst a burning town. Ronnie Van Zant proved irreplaceable. He had never been just a singer, he was the main songwriter, the image making front man, and to many people he was Lynyrd Skynyrd.

BELOW: *Ronnie Van Zant with Gary Rossington and Allen Collins. Lynyrd Skynyrd were the pride of the South.*

ALSO IN ROCK'N'ROLL HEAVEN

I n this book, we've concentrated mainly on the well-known rock stars who have passed away, but there are just as many lesser stars in rock'n'roll heaven; bassists and keyboard players of major league bands; members of less well-known groups; one-hit wonders lost in the rush of time and lead singers of bands that didn't quite make it. Here are a few who definitely warrant a mention.

The youngest person to be admitted into rock'n'roll heaven must be Ritchie Valens. In 1958 he had got to No. 2 in the charts with 'Donna/La Bamba' and was touring through the Mid-West with Buddy Holly when their plane went down. The seat that Ritchie was in was actually meant for Buddy's guitarist Tommy Allsup but Valens pestered the guitarist so much that in the end they flipped a coin and Ritchie got the seat. He was 17 years old.

LEFT: *Ritchie Valens had only just become famous when he died in 1958, in the same plane crash as Buddy Holly.*

OPPOSITE: *The Carpenters. Karen's death in 1982 was from heart trouble brought on by annorexia.*

ABOVE: *Frankie Lymon and the Teenagers. His high pre-adolescent voice was his trademark and when it broke he was in trouble. He had known fame at 13 and was a has-been by 17. He died in 1968.*

Someone who became a star at a younger age than Valens was Frankie Lymon. His song with The Teenagers, 'Why Do Fools Fall In Love' came out when he was only thirteen. It was his high, pre-pubescent voice that gave the record a lot of its appeal, and it's said that Diana Ross based her singing style around Lymon's voice. By the time Ross covered 'Why Do Fools Fall In Love' in 1981, Frankie had already been dead for 13 years. When his voice broke he fell out of favour and by 17 he was a washed-up drug addict. He kept trying to cure himself of addiction, going to various clinics, but he always returned to drugs and finally in 1968 he was found dead on his grandmother's bathroom floor.

A woman you certainly wouldn't have expected to be mingling with rock's hard-living casualties on the other side is Karen Carpenter. Karen's death in 1982 was not from drugs but from heart trouble caused by anorexia. Her death must be one of the most tragic in all rock'n'roll.

OPPOSITE ABOVE: *The Mamas and the Papas. Mama Cass (right) died of a heart attack in 1974.*

OPPOSITE BELOW: *The death of drummer John Bonham (left) in 1980 brought an end to one of the world's greatest rock bands.*

Members of English rock bands in rock'n'roll heaven include John Bonham, drummer of Led Zeppelin and Paul Kossoff, guitarist with Free. Chrissie Hynde's band The Pretenders suffered two losses in the space of two years. First to go was guitarist and co-songwriter James Honeyman-Scott who died in 1982, then bassist Pete Farndon went the following year. Both deaths were attributable to drugs.

Two West Coast casualties of the hippie era are Cass Elliot of The Mamas and The Papas who died in 1974 of a heart attack, and Ron 'Pigpen' McKernan, keyboard player of the Grateful Dead, whose death in 1973 was caused by a liver disease.

One of the most sordid of all rock'n'roll deaths and a possible suicide, was the death of Sex Pistol Sid Vicious in 1979. He had already killed his girlfriend Nancy Spungeon and was heard to say that he wanted to fulfil his side of a suicide pact. He died of a heroin overdose while awaiting trial.

ABOVE: *The Grateful Dead lost keyboard player, Ron 'Pigpen' McKernan in 1973. It wasn't a drug death but the result of a liver disease.*

LEFT: *The Pretenders. Both James Honeyman-Scott (2nd left) and Pete Farndon (end right) were to die within a year of each other. Both deaths were attributable to drugs.*

OPPOSITE: *Sid Vicious. He had an outrageous life capped off by an outrageous death. He committed suicide while awaiting trial for the murder of his girlfriend Nancy Spungeon.*

INDEX

Note: Many caption references are contained within textual references; otherwise caption references are in italics.

A

Ain't Misbehaving (Haley) 23
Ain't No Mountain High Enough (Gaye) 44, 46
Ain't Nothing Like the Real Thing (Gaye) 44, 46
airplane crashes 8, 88
 Jim Croce 78
 Buddy Holly 21
 Lynyrd Skynyrd 87
 Rick Nelson 35
 Otis Redding 43
alcohol 50, 62
Alexander, J.W. 41
Allison, Jerry 19
Allman, Duane 6, 8, 71–2, 86
Allman Gregg 71
Allsup Tommy 21, 88
Atlantic Records 33
Andrews, Sam 57
The Animals 60
Anka, Paul 21
Atkins, Chet 36
Aznageel the Mage (Bolan) 82

B

Bad Bad Leroy Brown (Croce) 78
Ball and Chain (Joplin) 56
Band of Gypsies 53
Be Bop Baby (Nelson) 34
Beach Boys 47–50
The Beatles 9, 33, 63–7, 83
Be-Bop-A-Lula (Vincent) 29
Beck, Jeff 52, 71
Bee Gees 84–5
Beecher, Francis *23*
Beggars Banquet (Jones) 62
Berry, Chuck 25, 60
Betts, Dickie 71
Big Bopper *see* Richardson, J.P.
Big Brother and the Holding Company 54, 57
Blackwell, Chris 73
Blue Moon of Kentucky (Presley) 15
Blue Suede Shoes (Presley) 15
Bolan, Marc 8, 80–3
Bonham, John *89*, 90
Booker, Cedella 73
Bowie, David 83
Brakespeare, Cindy 74
Brown, James 42
Brumley, Tom 34
Burnette, Johnny and Dorsey 34
Burning Love (Presley) 15
Burning (Marley) 74
Burton, James 34

C

cancer 74–5
Capaldi, Jim 68
Capehart, Jerry 27, 28
Capitol Records 72
car/motorcycle crashes 8, 37
 Duane Allman 71
 Marc Bolan 83
 Harry Chapin 77
 Eddie Cochran 28
Carpenter, Karen 6, *88*, 89
Carroll, Lewis 66
Cashman, Terry 78
Cass, Mama *see* Elliot
Cassotto, Robert Walden *see* Darin, Bobby
Catch A Fire (Marley) 74
Cat's in the Cradle (Chapin) 76
Chalpin, Ed 53
Chandler, Chas 51–2, 53
Chapin, Harry 8, 76–7
Chapman, Mark 67
Charles, Ray 33
Cheap Thrills (Joplin) 56
Clapton, Eric 52, 71
C'mon Everybody (Cochran) 25, 28
Cochran, Eddie 8, 10, 25–8, 30
Cochran, Hank 25
Cole, Nat King 44
Collins, Allen 86
The Comets *22*, 23–4
Conley, Arthur 43
Cook, Dale 39
Cooke, Sam 6, 9, 39–41, 42, 51

Costello, Elvis 38
Crazy Man Crazy (Haley) 22, 23
Cream 60
The Cricketts *18*, 19–21
Croce, Ingrid 78
Croce, Jim 8, 78–9
Crying (Orbison) 36, 37
Curtis, King 71
Curtis, Tony 33

D

Daltrey, Roger 68
The Dammed 83
Darin, Bobby 8, 31–3
Davis, Miles 53
Davis, Tex 29
Dean, James 12, 83
Decca Records 19, 31, 33
Dee, Sandra *32*, 33
Delaney and Bonnie 71
Dinah (Haley) 23
Dock of the Bay (Redding) 42, 43
Domino, Fats 8, 27, 28, 34
Donna/La Bamba (Valens) 88
Don't Back Down (Wilson) 47
Don't (Presley) 12, 16
The Doors 58–9
Dorsey, Tommy 76
Dowd, Tom 86
Dream Baby (Orbison) 36, 37
Dream Lover (Darin) 31, 33
drugs 8–9, 89, 90
 Marc Bolan 82

Jimi Hendrix 53
Janis Joplin 57
Keith Moon 70
Elvis Presley 17
Rolling Stones 62
Dennis Wilson 49
Dylan, Bob 38, 41, 53, 54

E

Electra recording company 76
Elliot, 'Mama' Cass 6, 9, 89, 90
Entwistle, John 68
Epstein, Brian 65, 66, 80
Ertegun, Ahmet 33
The Everly Brothers 36
Exodus (Marley) 73, 74
The Experience *8*

F

Fabian 29
Farndon, Pete 90, 92
Floyd, Eddie 42
Franklin, Aretha 71
Free Bird (Lynyrd Skynyrd) 86
Fuqua, Harvey 44
Fury, Billy *10*, 25

G

Gaines, Cassie 86, 87
Gaines, Steve 6, 8, 86, 87

Gallup, Cliff 29
Garden Party (Nelson) 34, 35
Gaye, Marvin 6, 44–6
Generation X 83
Gibb, Andy 84–5
The Girl Can't Help It (film) 27, 28
Girls On The Beach (Wilson) 47
Gordy, Anna 44, 46
Gordy, Berry 44
Gordy, Gwen 44
Grande, John *23*
Grateful Dead 58, 90
Grossman, Albert 54, 56
Guiltiness (Marley) 74

Haley, Bill 8, 9, 22–4
Harris, Rebert 39
Harrison, George 38
Heads and Tails (Chapin) 76
heart ailments/attacks 89, 90
  Bobby Darin 33
  Andy Gibb 84
  Bill Haley 24
  Roy Orbison 38
Heartbreak Hotel (Presley) 12, 15
Heathen (Marley) 74
Hello I Love You (Morrison) 58
Hendrix, Jimi 8, 9, 51–3, 71
Here My Dear (Gaye) 46
Herman, Woody 76
The Highway QC's 39
Holly, Buddy 8, 10, 18–21, 27, 34, 36, 88
Honeyman-Scott, James *11*, 90, 92
Hot Rod Gang (film) 30
Hot Rod Mama (Bolan) 82
Hounddog (Presley) 12, 15
How Sweet It Is (Gaye) 44, 46
Hynde, Chrissie 90

I Am the Walrus (Lennon) 66
I Got a Name (Croce) 78
I Heard It Through the Grapevine (Gaye) 44, 46
I Just Want Your Everything (Gibb) 84
I'm Walking (Nelson) 34
Inner City Blues (Gaye) 44, 46
Isle of Wight Festival 53
Isley Brothers 51
It Doesn't Matter Anymore (Holly) 18, 21
It's Late (Nelson) 34
It's Up to You (Nelson) 34

Jagger, Mick 60, 61, 62
Jailhouse Rock (Presley) 12, 16
Jefferson Airplane 43
Jennings, Waylon 21
John, Elton 83
Jones, Brian 6, 60–2
Jones, Gloria 83
Jones, Ralph *23*
Joplin, Janis 9, 54–7
Jumping Jack Flash (Jones) 60, 62

King, B.B. 51
King, Ben E. 41
King Creole (film) 16
King, Ed 86
The Kinks 60, 68
Kooper, Al 86
Kossoff, Paul 90

L.A. Woman (Morrison) 59
Lady Sings the Blues (film) 33
Layla (Allman) 71
Lennon, Cynthia 64, 67
Lennon, John 6, 9, 29, 63–7
Lennon, Julian 63, 67
Let's Get It On (Gaye) 44, 46
Lewis, Jerry Lee 8, 21, 36
Liberty Company 27
Life and Times (Croce) 78
Light My Fire (Morrison) 58
Little Richard 8, *27, 28,* 42
Livingstone, Bunny 73–4
London, Julie *27, 28*
Lonesome Town (Nelson) 34
Love is Thicker (Gibb) 84
Love, Mick 47, 50
The Luck of the Irish (Lennon) 67
Lymon, Frankie 7, 9, 89
Lynyrd Skynyrd 71, 86–7

McCartney, Paul 21, 52, 63, 65
Mack the Knife (Darin) 31, 33
McKernan, Ron 'Pigpen' 6, 90, *92*
Maisner, Randy 34
The Mamas and Papas 89
Manson, Charles 47, 49
Manzarek, Ray 58, 59
Marley, Bob 9, 73–5
Marley, Norval 73
Mayall, John 60
Meet Me at the Twistin' Place (Cooke) 41
Melcher, Terry 49
Melson, Joe 36
Mercy Mercy Me (Gaye) 44, 46
Midnight Love (Gaye) 44, 46
Milne, A.A. 62
Mitchell, Joni 76

Mitchell, Mitch *8*, 52
Monterey Pop Festival 43, 52, 54
Montgomery, Bob 19
Monument Records 36
Moon, Keith 6, 9, 68–70
Moon, Kim 70
Morgan, Seth 57
Morisette, Johnnie 41
Morrison, Jim 58–9
Motown 32, 44, 46
Muehleisen, Murray 78
Mustang Ford (Bolan) 82
My Generation (Moon) 68
My Heart (Vincent) 30
My People Were Fair and Had Sky In Their Hair But Now They're Content To Wear Stars On Their Brows (Bolan) 82
Mystery Girl (Orbison) 36, 38

Napier-Bell, Simon 80, 83
Nelson, Harriet 34, *35*
Nelson, Ken 29
Nelson, Ozzie 34
Nelson, Rick 8, 29, 34–5
Nilsson, Harry 70

Page, Jimmy 71
Pallenberg, Anita 62
Parker, Col. 15–17
Peck, Gregory 33
Peel, John 83
Peggy Sue (Holly) 18, 19
Petty, Norman 19, 21
Petty, Tom 38
Phillips, Sam 15, 36
Pickett, Wilson 39, 71
Piece of My Heart (Joplin) 54, 56
Pistol Packin' Mama (Vincent) 30
Plastic Ono Band 67
Poitier, Sidney *31*
Pompelli, Rudy *23*, 24
Poor Little Fool (Nelson) 34
Presley, Elvis 9, 12–17, 18, 23, 27, 28, 33, 34, 36, 41, 51, 63
Presley, Priscilla 17
Presley, Vernon 14
Pressure Point (film) *31*
The Pretenders 9, *11*, 90, *92*

Q

Quadrephenia (Moon) 70
The Quarrymen 63
Queen of the Hop (Darin) 31, 33

R

RCA 14, 15, 36
Redding, Noel *8*, 52
Redding, Otis 6, 8, 9, 42–3, 71
Reeves, Martha 44
Respect (Redding) 42
Rex, Al *23*
Rich, Buddy 70
Richards, Keith 60, 61, 62

Richardson, J.P. 21
Ride a White Swan (Bolan) 80, 82
Riders on the Storm (Morrison) 58, 59
Rimbaud, Arthur 59
Robinson, Smokey 44
Rock Around the Clock (Haley) 22, 23
Rolling Stones 42, 60–2
Ross, Diana 89
Rossington, Gary 86
Running Scared (Orbison) 36, 37
Rush, Otis 71

S

The Saddlemen 22–3
Salamanda Palaganda (Bolan) 82
Santiago, Maria Elena 21
SAR recording company 41
Satisfaction (Jones) 60
Scaggs, Boz 71
Second Helping (Lynyrd Skynyrd) 86
Sexual Healing (Gaye) 44, 46
Shadow Dancing (Gibb) 84
Sheeley, Sharon 28, 30
shootings
  Sam Cooke 41
  Marvin Gaye 46
  John Lennon 67
Sid Vicious 9, 90, *92*
Sinatra, Frank 33, 44
Sittin' in the Balcony (Cochran) 28
Skinner, Leonard 86
So Much Things To Say (Marley) 74
Spector, Phil 65, 67
Splish Splash (Darin) 31, 33
Springsteen, Bruce 38
Spungeon, Nancy 90, *92*
Stand By Me Father (Cooke) 41
Stanwyck, Barbara *9*

Starr, Ringo 70
Stewart, Rod 83
Stood Up (Nelson) 34
Stubborn Kind of Fellow (Gaye) 44
Stuck on You (Presley) 12, 16
Summertime Blues (Cochran) 25, 28
Sun Records 14, 15
Sunday Bloody Sunday (Lennon) 67
Surfer Girl (Wilson) 47
Surfin' USA (Wilson) 47
Sweet Home Alabama (Lynyrd Skynyrd) 86
Sweet Sue Just You (Haley) 23

T

Taylor, Don 74
Taylor, James 76
The Teenagers (Lymon) 89
Terrell, Tammi 46
That'll Be the Day (Holly) 18, 19
That's Alright Mama (Presley) 15
Three Steps to Heaven (Cochran) 25, 28
Time in a Bottle (Croce) 78
Tommy (Moon) 70
Took, Steve Peregrine 80–2
Tosh, Peter 73, 74
Townshend, Pete 52, 68
Trelawyn Lawn (Bolan) 82
The Twist 23
Two Virgins (Lennon) 67
Tyrannosaurus Rex 82

V

Valens, Ritchie 8, 10, 21, 88, 89
Van Zant, Ronnie 6, 8, 86, 87
Vincent, Gene 8, 9, *27*, 28, 29–30

W

The Wailers 73–4
Walden, Phil 71
Waters, Muddy 60
Wells, Mary 44
West Coast Imperial Records 34
West, Tommy 78
Weston, Mary 46
What's Going On (Gaye) 44, 46
The Who 43, 68–70, 86
Why Do Fools Fall in Love (Lymon) 89
Williams, Billy *23*
Wilson, Brian 47, 50
Wilson, Carl 47
Wilson, Carol 47
Wilson, Dennis 47–50
Wilson, Jackie 51
Woman is the Nigger of the World (Lennon) 67
Woman (Lennon) 63
Wonderful World (Cooke) 39, 42

Y

Yoko Ono 66–7
You Get It (Orbison) 36, 38
You Send Me (Cooke) 39, 41
Young, Neil 86
Young World (Nelson) 34
You're The Reason I'm Living (Darin) 31, 33

Z

Zimbabwe (Marley) 74

Acknowledgements: *all photographs PICTORIAL PRESS, except 76, 77, 78, 79, 86, 87, 92 (below), REX FEATURES*